D0845072

FREE

AND

SWISS

GEORG THÜRER

FREE
AND
SWISS

THE STORY
OF SWITZERLAND

*Adapted and translated
from the German by*
R. P. HELLER & E. LONG

—

University of Miami Press
Coral Gables, Florida

First published in Switzerland
in 1948 under the title *Bundesspiegel*
by Artemis Verlags-Ag, Zürich

First English edition Copyright © 1970
by Oswald Wolff (Publishers) Limited, London

American edition Copyright © 1971
by University of Miami Press

Library of Congress Catalog Card Number 73-170140

ISBN 0-87024-229-6

Manufactured in the United States of America

CONTENTS

LIST OF MAPS AND ILLUSTRATIONS

Photographs from:
Swiss National Tourist Office, Zurich: 1
H. Schönwetter, Glarus: 2
Kunstmuseum Winterthur: 3
Bibliothèque de Genève: 4
Graphische Sammlung der Zentralbibliothek, Zurich: 5, 6, 7
Freddy Bertrand, Geneva: 8
Schweizerisches Rotes Kreuz, Pressedienst, Bern: 9
Office Suisse d'Expansion Commerciale, Lausanne: 10
W. Studer, Berne: 11
Hans Steiner, Berne: 12

TRANSLATORS' NOTE

This adaptation of Professor Thürer's history of Switzerland is based on the author's expanded and revised German edition of 1964 and contains further material on events since then. For the benefit of English-speaking readers, the translators have also drawn on additional sources to fill in the background of Swiss history and to provide more detail about the way the country is governed and its economic life. Professor Thürer's book, entitled *Bundesspiegel*, was originally written for the centenary of the federal state in 1948 and soon became a popular handbook in Swiss homes and schools. The translators wish to thank him for his co-operation and would also like to acknowledge their debt to Dr. Paul Stauffer, Cultural Attaché at the Swiss Embassy in London, for his unstinting help and constructive advice in the preparation of this edition.

London, December 1969.   E. L.
                                                                        R. P. H.

I

The People and The Land

I SETTING THE SCENE

THE WAY the Swiss have created unity out of diversity is a central theme of their entire history. Their country, with its contrasting regions, does not have the benefit of well-defined natural boundaries, and there is no single language or religion to hold the people together. Moreover, the unifying force of a dominant ruling group has been lacking, and even when all Europe was governed by monarchs the Swiss were republicans. Their struggle for independence began among the peasant farmers of the Alpine valleys in the heart of the country, gradually spreading outwards to embrace more and more neighbouring communities until a federal state was developed, taking its name from one of the original members, the tiny canton of Schwyz. In this process, spanning many centuries, the individual characteristics of different regional and language groups were not eliminated but encouraged. Each made its own contribution to the common aim of a greater harmony, as the nations of western Europe as a whole are learning to do in their search for integration.

Switzerland's position in modern Europe is, of course, in certain respects exceptional. The country's neutrality in the great wars marked it out as different from its neighbours, and more fortunate. General respect for this neutrality meant that it was spared the suffering and destruction that other countries experienced. Even in times of the greatest turmoil during this century, it has managed to remain relatively stable, and this stability has contributed to its prosperity and to its emergence as a great financial and commercial centre. Peace and tolerance have made it a haven for refugees. The beauty of its landscape has attracted countless tourists. But only the scenery is a gift of nature. The peace, prosperity and stability of the country, like its unification, have been accomplished in the face of obstacles which a closer study makes immediately apparent.

Modern Switzerland is a Confederation of 22 cantons, with historically conditioned differences in language and religion. Under the constitution, even in this age of big units and centralised power, the cantons still retain considerable autonomy and cherish the right to make their voices heard. Since three of them first came together in a freely-contracted union in the 13th century, the history of the country has essentially been the history of cantonal development. Progress and reform have been rooted in the cantons, and unity has depended on their willingness to sink their differences even after such disasters as civil war.

The diversity of the cantons reflects the country's linguistic and religious composition. Four languages—German, French, Italian and Romansh—are spoken among the total population of six millions. Romansh, despite its relative obscurity, is recognised under the constitution as a national language, although it is not compulsory for official purposes as the others are. German is the majority language in 16 of the cantons, French in five, and Italian in one. Taking the nation as a whole, including foreign residents, the language breakdown as shown in the last census of 1960 is as follows: German speakers, approximately 69 per cent; French, 19 per cent; Italian, 9·5 per cent; Romansh, 1 per cent. A similar break-down for religion shows that approximately 53 per cent are Protestants and 46 per cent Catholics. The cantons are about equally divided between those with Protestant and Catholic majorities.

Religious loyalties do not coincide with linguistic divisions, and both in fact cut across cantonal boundaries. Thus the canton of Berne has a large number of French speakers although its predominant language is German. And the city of Lucerne, though in the strongly Catholic central area of the country, has a considerable Protestant minority.

Religious bigotry is a thing of the past in Switzerland, although like other peoples the Swiss have had to learn the importance of tolerance in the hard school of historical development. Freedom of conscience and creed is guaranteed in the constitution, and the state regards religious belief as a private matter for the individual. As for the linguistic divisions, although German is the predominant language in a majority of the cantons, particularly those in the north and centre, neither political influence nor civic rights are based in any way on language.

Until one sees how the problems have been solved by the modern Confederation, four languages and two major religious faiths seem an unlikely basis for national unity such as the Swiss have achieved. Equally, the country's geography does not provide a promising foundation for economic and political development. When it comes to natural resources, Switzerland has little but its magnificent scenery and a wealth of water power, vitally important though both have been to certain aspects of its economy. Industry was built up on water power; the mountains attracted tourists with money to spend; but ingenuity and determination were required to compensate for the lack of raw materials in constructing the progressive industrial and trading nation that modern Switzerland has become.

The fundamental feature of the country's geography is its land-locked position in the centre of western Europe; and this has had an important bearing on its entire history. The challenge is plain from the map, and until our day it has been formidable. Here is a small nation, composed of the most diverse elements and determined to retain its tradition of independence, but hemmed in by four countries which for long periods down the centuries were centres of power and aggrandizement: France, Germany, Italy and Austria. Moreover, Switzerland's key position on traditional north-south routes across Europe has given it strategic importance since the Romans crossed the Alps. These factors have influenced the country's economic and political development at every stage, and without a full appreciation of their importance nothing about it can be truly understood. They played their part in the creation of a unified Confederation; in its decision to adopt permanent neutrality in order to protect its very existence; and during modern times even in its reluctance to join the United Nations for fear of sacrificing that neutrality.

Switzerland's landlocked borders enclose a total area of 15,941 square miles. Of this, about three-fifths is taken up by the Alpine region which stretches in all its spectacular beauty right across the country, reaching its summit in the Dufour Peak of Monte Rosa, 15,217 feet high. The head-waters of great rivers collect in the valleys of the Alps: the Rhine, which flows for 235 miles through

Switzerland before heading north through Germany; the Rhone, which reaches France 165 miles from its source in the Rhone Glacier of the Alps; the Inn, which leaves the mountains of eastern Switzerland eventually to feed the great Danube; and the Ticino, flowing south from the Gotthard to join the Po in Italy. Innumerable other rivers and lakes make water transport a vital factor in Swiss history: together with the Alpine passes, the water routes have been an important strategic consideration both in peace and war, not just for the Swiss themselves but for their neighbours.

To the north of the Alps, the scenery changes from mountains to hills and open fields. This is the plateau, extending north-eastwards for 150 miles from Lake Geneva to Lake Constance; and it is here that the main cities are found. The entire lowlands of Switzerland, however, account for less than a third of the country's area, and towards the French border the land rises again into the mountains of the Jura, lower than the Alps and less dramatic, but with their own particular beauty.

To the south of the Alps, there is change again: the milder climate of the Italian-speaking Ticino area on the route that throughout history has taken armies and travellers to Italy and the Mediterranean. To the stranger, Locarno and Lugano seem almost to be parts of another country, such is the difference in atmosphere in comparison with the north. Yet all these complex strands of geography, language, religion and cultural tradition are held together in one nation. The Ticinese themselves summed it up in a battle cry they used when they were struggling for liberty in the Napoleonic era. The cry was *Liberi e Svizzeri,* demonstrating in the historical context their determination to make their future with the rest of Switzerland in preference to the alternatives offered to them. What the Ticinese proclaimed in their slogan "Free and Swiss" has been true of Switzerland's history throughout the ages: the Confederation was born of the determination of the cantons to defend their liberty, and the Swiss have always shown their resolve to remain free citizens of a free country.

II THE ORIGINS OF THE PEOPLE

The story of Switzerland begins in the mountains, rather than in the lowlands where most of the population lives today. It was beneath sheltering rock-faces high up in the Alps that the country's first inhabitants made their appearance about 100,000 years ago.

Between the last two Ice Ages, a race of hunters is known to have already used the Wildkirchli cave, more than 4,500 feet up in the Appenzellerland, the Drachenloch, 8,000 feet high in the Oberland of St. Gallen, and mountain caves in other regions. No physical remains of them have been preserved, but archaeologists base their knowledge on other discoveries. Primitive tools have been found, and coloured stones which must have been carried up from the valleys by cavemen who delighted in their beauty and used them as ornaments. In the Drachenloch, an even more curious clue was brought to light : skulls of cave-bears that had been carefully stacked in stone containers possibly 100,000 years ago, and which some scholars regard as the first monument to man's awakening belief in a god.

Life was an unending struggle up there near the tree-line, still known as the battle-zone, *die Kampfzone*. But already in the Old Stone Age, man's first weapons and tools helped him to kill game, to brighten the darkness with a torch of flame, to light a fire to warm his cave, and to build a rough stone wall at its entrance to protect his children from falling to their death over a precipice. The wall outside the Wildkirchli cave, in fact, is believed to be the oldest stonework yet discovered on earth.

The early people of the Alps did not survive the perils of the advancing glaciers as the Ice Ages progressed; but man reappeared in the mountains at the time of the last great melting of the glaciers, settling in the northern region which was the first to be free of ice. Pictorial evidence of human endeavour about 15,000 years ago has been found in the mountain caves of the Jura near Schaffhausen : it is a drawing of a grazing reindeer, scratched onto a bone and showing the artistry with which these primitive people tried to portray the world around them.

By the time of the New Stone Age, the glaciers had receded further and allowed access to the fertile plateau. On the lake shores, villages of log huts were erected, supported on piles. These celebrated lake villages were at one time always pictured rising idyllically from the waters; but opinion today is that most of them were on firm ground and that piles were mainly used to prevent them from being swamped when the water level rose. From these raised settlements, the people could keep watch on their surrounding fields and the grazing animals they had tamed; they could harvest a rich catch of fish from the lakes; and as fishermen and craftsmen they are known to have made nets as well as cloth.

Metal goods, the next evidence of man's ingenuity, first reached Switzerland from the Mediterranean lands by way of barter. In the Bronze Age (1800–800 B.C.) the people still depended on imported tin and copper to make bronze; but in the ensuing early Iron Age they were probably able to smelt iron ore in their own furnaces. At this time the high Alps and their foothills were virtually uninhabited, while the population was increasing in the Jura and the plateau; and in the late Iron Age (from 500 B.C.) there emerged a great new centre of culture on the north bank of Lake Neuchâtel. This was La Tène, the site which has given its name to a whole period of civilisation enriched by the beauty of Celtic art. The Celtic peoples expanded across a large part of Europe, but in the end their way of life declined in the face of Roman power. Later, in the early Middle Ages, it was left to Celtic Ireland to provide a link between the La Tène civilisation in Switzerland and the world of the Christian missionaries. But before then, Rome had spread its government, culture and language to the Swiss regions and the Germanic tribes had made their appearance.

*   *   *

The earliest written records about Switzerland date back to the pre-Christian era, and show that then as now the land was not inhabited by a homogeneous population. In the west and north ever since the later Bronze Age there had lived a Celtic people known as the Helvetii. Bordering them in the east were the Raeti, presumably of Illyrian-Venetian extraction; while in the south the people were of a Ligurian strain.

Shortly before the Christian era, the Helvetii decided to migrate to the coast-lands of south-west Gaul, already familiar to other Celtic people. Not only did the Helvetii yearn for more living space for their sizeable population, but they also sought safety from the threat of the Germanic tribesmen who were pressing on their borders. The migration was inspired by a member of the nobility, Orgetorix, who appar-

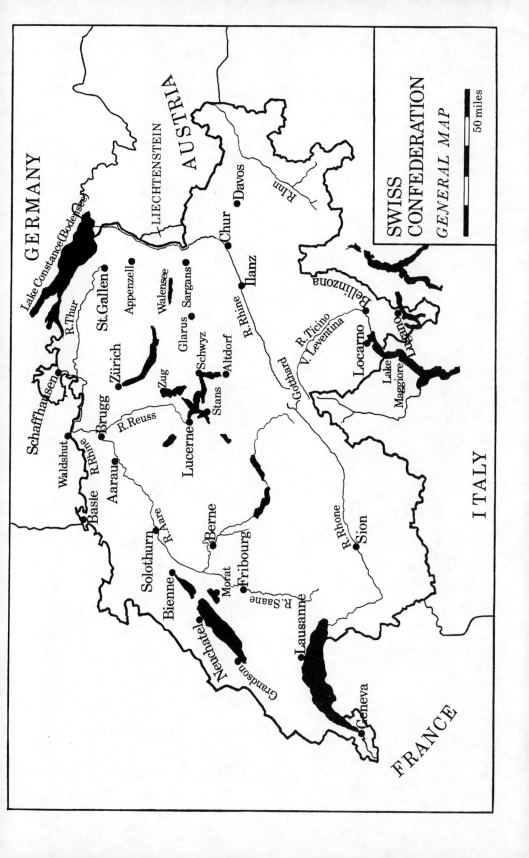

SWISS
CONFEDERATION
GENERAL MAP

50 miles

GERMANY

AUSTRIA

LIECHTENSTEIN

ITALY

FRANCE

Lake Constance (Bodensee)

R. Thur

Schaffhausen

Waldshut

R. Rhine

Basle

Aarau

R. Reuss

R. Aare

Solothurn

Brugg

Zürich

St. Gallen

Appenzell

Walensee

Glarus Sargans

Schwyz

Zug

Stans

Lucerne

Altdorf

R. Rhine

Ilanz

Chur

Davos

R. Inn

Berne

Bienne

Morat

Fribourg

Neuchatel

Grandson

R. Saane

Lausanne

Geneva

Sion

R. Rhone

Gotthard

V. Leventina

R. Ticino

Locarno

Lake
Maggiore

Lugano

Bellinzona

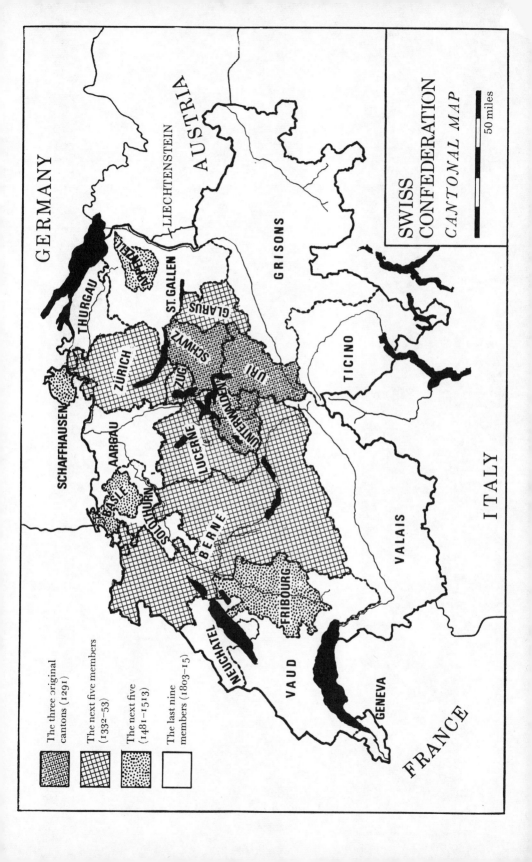

GERMANY

AUSTRIA

LIECHTENSTEIN

THURGAU

APPENZELL

SCHAFFHAUSEN

ST. GALLEN

GLARUS

ZÜRICH

SCHWYZ

GRISONS

ZUG

AARGAU

URI

UNTERWALDEN

LUCERNE

TICINO

BASLE

SOLOTHURN

BERNE

VALAIS

FRIBOURG

NEUCHATEL

VAUD

GENEVA

ITALY

FRANCE

SWISS
CONFEDERATION
CANTONAL MAP

50 miles

The three original
cantons (1291)

The next five members
(1332–53)

The next five
(1481–1513)

The last nine
members (1803–15)

ently hoped that its success would enable him to establish a Helvetian monarchy with himself on the throne. The tribe had, in fact, long since dispensed with kingship, and when this attempt to restore it was revealed Orgetorix chose suicide rather than suffer death at the stake, which was the penalty for trying to establish autocratic rule.

Despite this crisis, the Helvetii were still determined to find new lands for settlement: but Rome barred their advance. When they attempted to make their way to the south-west by taking a route through the area of Geneva, Julius Caesar refused them permission to cross Roman territory. The Helvetian horde therefore surged over the Jura further north, but they were pursued by Caesar's army and defeated in battle at Bibracte near Autun in the year 58 B.C. Those who survived were forced to return to their former lands and rebuild the towns and villages they had burned before leaving. Caesar nevertheless granted the Helvetii favourable conditions as privileged allies of Rome, for he needed them to help guard the Rhine against the threat from Germanic tribes in the north. Soon they adapted their way of life to that of their Roman masters; and in 15 B.C. the Raeti, a barbarous and warlike people, were also defeated and incorporated into the Roman Empire.

For about ten generations the country enjoyed peace, the *Pax Romana*. Rome brought an administrative and economic system which was more elaborate and sophisticated than anything the Helvetii had known, and they were by no means reluctant to adopt its refinements. The outcome, however, was a regional civilisation rather than a purely Roman one, for the Celtic people had much to contribute themselves from their own culture and traditions. In the society which developed, their agricultural knowledge, organisational skill and experience of self-government all played a part. They themselves had built some simple roads as well as towns; now, under the influence of Rome, the road system was extended and several large towns flourished, such as Aventicum (Avenches) near Lake Neuchâtel, Augusta Raurica (Kaiseraugst) near present-day Basle, and the important garrison town of Vindonissa (Windisch) between the rivers Aare and Reuss, the strongest frontier fortress of the time. The towns had their amphitheatres, temples and thermal baths, and in the country the villas with mosaic floors, glass windows and warm-air heating offered a comfortable mode of life for the better-off provincials. Merchants and

officials, soldiers, builders and priests came over the mountain passes
from the south, bringing with them the culture and language of
Roman civilisation.

In language as in other ways, the 500 years or so of Roman rule
left a much stronger imprint on Switzerland than on its south German
neighbours, for whom Rome's dominion lasted only about half as
long. The Roman past is seen in the Latin roots of three of
the national languages of the country: French, spoken mainly in the
west, Italian in the south, and the minority language Romansh, which
is spoken today only by about 50,000 people in the eastern canton of
the Grisons, the descendants of refugees who fled to safety during
the Germanic invasions which finally brought an end to Roman
power.

The coming of the Germanic tribes, like the rule of Rome, left an
enduring mark on the history and linguistic pattern of Switzerland.
Even the development of a Latin language such as French was influenced by the arrival of the Germanic Burgundians, who settled in
the west of Switzerland. But they were relatively few in number, and
were assimilated into the native life. In the northern and central areas,
which were in any event less Romanised, the invasion of a more
dominant Germanic tribe, the Alemanni, had a decisive effect on the
future of what was to become German-speaking Switzerland. Already
in the 3rd century, the Alemanni had staged daring raids across the
Rhine, destroying the city of Aventicum. The raids continued, and
although the Romans managed to hold the line for a century and
more, there was no withstanding the eventual mass migration.

                    *   *   *

The Alemanni may be described as the forerunners of the Swiss
Confederation in the sense that its original members in the Alpine
lands had no noteworthy roots in the Romano-Celtic civilisation and
inherited the Germanic traditions. Study of the period shows that the
Alemanni were an association of tribes who demonstrated their
opposition to central rule and conformity in the way they conducted their public affairs. There were, of course, noblemen, free-
men, bondsmen and slaves; but the political centre of gravity was the
people's assembly, the precursor of the *Landsgemeinde* which was to
play such an important part in the future development of the can-

tons. In their economic and social organisation, the Alemanni also
had a profound influence on their successors. When the occupation
and distribution of territory by Alemannian families began in the late
5th century, not all the land was divided into farmsteads. A large
part, the *Allmende,* belonged to the community as a whole, and all
had grazing rights on it. Majority decision governed all matters
affecting the common land, such as rights of way, the use of streams,
and the construction of bridges; and the common good took precedence over private interest.*

It was the Alemanni, therefore, who laid the foundations of the
democratic village life in which the future Confederation was to be
rooted; and their tradition of co-operation between individual and
community was to influence both the Confederation itself and the
Swiss character. The Alemannian past is also reflected in the German-
Swiss dialects, *Schwyzertütsch,* the everyday tongue among people of
all classes in German-speaking Switzerland today. This is more than
just ordinary dialect: for while literary German is used for writing,
Schwyzertütsch is the national spoken language.

*   *   *

The Germanic invasions temporarily halted the Christian mission
to Switzerland, which had begun from the south across the Alps and
along the Roman roads. When the Alemanni were becoming established, there were already bishoprics in existence in several parts of
the country, among them Augst (A.D. 346), Chur (451) and Constance
(about 600) on the Rhine, and St. Maurice (381) and Geneva (about
400) on the Rhone. These were the early foundations in a time of
transition; but Switzerland's final conversion was due to the work of
a group of Celtic missionaries led by St. Columbanus, who came south
to continental Europe from Ireland. Columbanus was a great founder
of monastic houses and quite indefatigable as a Christian teacher. In
course of time, the gospel gradually made its influence felt on the
lives of the Alemanni, and those who were baptised into the faith
brought a new element into the economic and legal community which
their people had created. This was the legacy of the Celtic mission,

---

* Numerous place names recall this period of Swiss history. Those ending
with "ingen" indicate early settlements; those ending with "ighofen" or "ikon"
later ones; and the final syllable "wil" denotes a yet later type.

and the country's debt to it is symbolised in the later choice of the
cross as the Swiss emblem.

Columbanus's pioneering work in Swiss territory was accomplished
in the early 7th century, and he later departed for Italy. But when
he left, his disciple Gallus was too ill to travel and stayed behind in
the solitude of a forest cell. This hermitage, founded in 612, became
the nucleus of the Benedictine monastery of St. Gallen, which by the
9th and 10th centuries was unequalled in the Germanic lands for art
and learning, with a monastery school that was a forerunner of
Europe's universities. During that period the great men of St. Gallen
included the poet Notker Balbulus and the musician and liturgist
Tuotilo; and some of the superbly illuminated manuscripts that have
come down to us from St. Gallen can still be seen in the Abbey
library.

III The Empire and the Rise of the Habsburgs

The most powerful of the Germanic tribes to emerge from the migra-
tions into Roman territory were the Franks, who finally overshadowed
their neighbours. Already about the year 500 they inflicted defeat on
the Alemanni, and later they continued their expansion until they
reached the zenith of their power under the great king of the west,
Charlemagne. The year 800 saw the revival of the title Roman
Emperor when Charlemagne was crowned by Pope Leo III at the
end of Christmas mass in St. Peter's. This symbolic ceremony brought
ruler and Church into a relationship of profound importance for the
later history of the Middle Ages. It also gave apparent substance to
the dream of a new Empire to inherit the majesty of Rome.

The Holy Roman Empire was a tribute to Charlemagne's personality and to his tremendous territorial achievement. The Frankish
dominions stretched across western Europe from the river Elbe to
Spain, and down into Italy. They included the whole of the territory
of Switzerland, whose history was to be so closely linked to the Empire
until the 15th century.

The Empire was divided, however, within 30 years of Charlemagne's death in 814. By the Treaty of Verdun in 843, it was shared
among his three grandsons, and was later split between two of them.
Switzerland was again politically divided, for the frontier between

the western and eastern kingdoms ran along the river Aare. It was not until 1032 that the Swiss territories were once more brought under a single ruler, Emperor Conrad II.

Conquest, diplomacy and marriage might strengthen an Emperor's position, but the Empire was beset by divisions which grew from its very nature. The equivocal relationship between ruler and Pope, and the increasing conflict of interest between them, brought about centuries of strife from which Switzerland in particular suffered, with its strategically placed passes on the route from the Rhine to Rome. The Empire was weakened, moreover, by the traditional elective system, which robbed it of the advantages of hereditary kingship and gave rise to discord among the princes involved in electing the Emperor. This sometimes brought war, further undermining imperial authority and feeding the ambitions and independent instincts of the princes, who were often more powerful in fact than the Empire itself.

The forces of imperial disintegration were also strengthened by feudalism. In its military aspects, feudalism basically arose from the need of medieval rulers to be certain of the allegiance of a strong force of horsemen. The knights, who received landed grants from conquered territory in reward for armed service, also thereby acquired administrative functions and privileges which were a source of profit and power. The growing influence of noble families merely increased their appetite for yet more power, until a whole principality was theirs. On such foundations were built the fortunes of the houses of Savoy, Zähringen, Kyburg, Toggenburg—and, above all, Habsburg, whose ancestral castle the *Habichtsburg* (the Castle of the Hawk) stood beside the river Aare in Switzerland. The Habsburgs were destined to become the mightiest dynasty in the west and to secure dominance over the Holy Roman Empire.

*   *   *

The Habsburgs first assumed the imperial crown in the second half of the 13th century. On the death in 1250 of the last great member of the Hohenstaufen dynasty, Frederick II, the Empire seemed to be more shadow than substance, and in the Great Interregnum that followed there was no effective ruler. The supporters of law and order began to look for an Emperor who would restore peace to the imperial territories, and in this situation the electoral princes finally chose Count Rudolf of Habsburg, who was born in 1218.

The active and ambitious Rudolf accepted the crown in 1273. The coronation at Aachen, where he took his place on the throne of Charlemagne, reflected the new glory of the Empire and of the Habsburgs themselves. On the evening of the coronation, two of Rudolf's daughters were married to influential princes; a third was destined to become Queen of Bohemia; and a fourth occupied the throne of Naples. Within a few years, in 1278, Rudolf's armies defeated his rival Ottokar of Bohemia, and he was in a position to hand over the territories of Styria and Austria to his sons Albert and Rudolf. By this step, the Habsburgs established their Danubian monarchy which remained a major power until 1918.

King Rudolf was convinced that he had an answer to the past weaknesses of the Empire : he believed that an imperial ruler should accumulate great dynastic power in order to keep both internal and external enemies in check. In seeking to expand and strengthen his family wealth and influence, however, he often ignored the distinction between imperial and family possessions, and tended to appoint administrators of his own private estates to offices under the crown. It was this that brought the Habsburgs into collision with the people of central Switzerland.

Communities which had hitherto supplied administrators from their own midst as *Reichsvögte*—imperial bailiffs—found that Rudolf filled the posts with outsiders who would loyally obey his orders. His aim was to restrict communal liberty in the interests of central control, and in general he succeeded. But the Alpine peasantry around Lake Lucerne met this policy with stubborn resistance in their determination to defend communal rights. Their independent attitude in the face of Habsburg bureaucracy led to a struggle from which the Swiss Confederation was born.

2

The Early Confederation

URING THE reign of Rudolf of Habsburg, as in the time of the Romans, the Alpine passes were a key to trade, communications and military power. Control of the passes was a vital step in the expansion of empire. For the mountain people themselves, the challenge was of a different order: their very existence depended on coming to terms with their formidable surroundings, and experience taught them that only common effort would bridge the torrents, provide defences against avalanches, and build tracks through the mountains. One of the greatest achievements of their society at the beginning of the 13th century was the construction of the pass across the St. Gotthard, a task which Roman builders had not accomplished.

Around the year 1200 the first iron girders of the Devil's Bridge were driven into the granite at the Schöllenen gorge. The Swiss owe a great deal of their liberty to the successful spanning of the gorge and to the skill and tenacity of the unknown bridge-builder. For the triumph of iron over rock was more than a superb technical achievement. By opening up the St. Gotthard pass, it was an epoch-making event in the country's history, establishing the shortest route between the two great centres of European trade, Flanders and Lombardy. With its numerous approach routes, the pass enabled a crossing of the Alps to be made in one single ascent and descent. In addition, for nearly a third of the distance from Lake Lucerne to Sesto Calende, at the southern end of Lake Maggiore, water transport could be used for both passengers and goods. The whole development was of tremendous importance, above all to the community of Uri, south of Lake Lucerne. From a remote cul-de-sac, the valley of Uri had become an indispensable link in an international traffic artery to Italy.

It was inevitable that Emperor Frederick II, the last Hohenstaufen ruler, would try to seize control of this north-south route during his struggle with the Pope in the first half of the 13th century. The Emperor had, however, pawned his protective authority over Uri to the Habsburgs, and now had to retrieve it if his strategic plans were to be accomplished. So as to escape Habsburg overlordship, the people of the valley offered the Emperor the money to have the pawn redeemed. In appreciation of this gesture, Uri was granted an important privilege in 1231, and one that was to have far-reaching consequences. From now on, the valley community was to remain directly subject only to the Empire: the Emperor was legally the immediate overlord of Uri.

At the time of the Great Interregnum, in the absence of effective imperial power, this change gave the people of Uri virtual independence; and in 1240, the same privilege was granted to their neighbour Schwyz, so removing it too from Habsburg control. The two communities maintained their own law and order and became accustomed to self-rule. But the process was interrupted when the Interregnum came to an end with the election of Rudolf of Habsburg as Emperor. Instead of finding a protector on the imperial throne, the Swiss were faced with an enemy of their liberty.

The prospect now was that the Habsburgs would strengthen their position in the *Waldstätte,* the forest communities of Uri, Schwyz, Obwalden and Nidwalden, grouped around the Vierwaldstättersee— Lake Lucerne. The communities—which in due course came to be known as the forest cantons—foresaw the danger that the Habsburgs would continue to whittle down their liberty, and knew the time had come for a crucial decision. Were they to retain the ancient rights of free peasant communities or gradually sink into subjection? Resistance stood a chance of success only if they took joint action. The moment of decision, according to the historian, Professor Karl Meyer, came in 1273, the year Rudolf of Habsburg succeeded to the imperial throne. Led, it seems, by a young judge from the Schwyz valley, Rudolf Stauffacher, the communities of Uri, Schwyz and Nidwalden concluded a secret alliance. They presumably incorporated in this agreement common principles for the preservation of peace in their lands. In any event, this union of the three valleys marked the birth of the Swiss Confederation.

Rudolf of Habsburg had recognised Uri as a direct dependency of the Empire, but not Schwyz. He maintained that the latter's privilege was invalid in law because it had been issued by Frederick II while he was under the ban of the Church during his dispute with the Pope. The people of Schwyz tried to make Rudolf change his mind by supplying him with 1,500 men for his army. Not only was this gesture unavailing, but within 18 months the Emperor ignored the community's ancient rule that free men should be judged by their peers; and he appointed a judge (*Talrichter*) of unfree origin to exercise jurisdiction over Schwyz. Faced with such attempts to tighten the Habsburg grip, the secret alliance was put to the test. In mid-July 1291, Rudolf died at Speyer on the Rhine; and as soon as the news of his death reached the shores of Lake Lucerne, the three communities went into action. Their popular assemblies—the *Landsgemeinden*—met and at the beginning of August renewed the original union by putting their seals to the Treaty of Alliance of 1291.

In the Treaty of Everlasting Alliance, as it is known, Uri, Schwyz and Nidwalden express their aims in these memorable words:

"The people of the valley of Uri, the community of the valley of Schwyz, and the community of Nidwalden, seeing the malice of the times, have solemnly agreed and bound themselves by oath to aid and defend each other with all their might and main, with their lives and property, both within and without their boundaries, each at his own expense, against every enemy whatever who shall attempt to molest them, either singly or collectively.

"Whoever hath a lord, let him obey him according to his bounden duty. We have unanimously decreed that we will accept no judge in our valleys who shall have obtained his office for a price, or who is not a native and resident among us. Every difference among the confederates shall be decided by their wisest men; and whoever shall reject their award shall be compelled by the other confederates.

"Whoever shall wilfully commit a murder shall suffer death, and he who shall attempt to screen the murderer from justice shall be banished from the valleys. An incendiary shall lose his privileges as a free member of the community, and whoever harbours him shall make good the damage. Whoever robs or molests another shall make full restitution out of the property he possesses.

"Everyone shall acknowledge the authority of a judge in either of the valleys. If internal quarrels arise, and one of the parties shall refuse fair satisfaction, the confederates shall support the other party.

"This covenant, for the common weal, shall, God willing, endure for ever."

The Everlasting Alliance of August 1291, annually commemorated by festivities throughout Switzerland, is profoundly significant as the basis of law and justice in the communities. Uri, Schwyz and Nidwalden—soon joined by Obwalden*—make it clear that they consider no sacrifice too great in the fight against oppression. They are determined to uphold the law and organise their social order themselves: respect for the law is in fact the chief feature of the treaty. Feuds and vengeance are to give way to the process of justice, and no wealthy man is to be allowed arbitrarily to seize a poor man's belongings or force him to pay money without a judge's permission. Nevertheless, the provision that a man must serve his master faithfully shows that the alliance was not conceived to promote revolution but to preserve the peace of the land at a time of trouble and uncertainty.

Study of the original parchment of the treaty, which is still kept in the federal archives at Schwyz, reveals one exceptionally interesting detail: throughout, the Latin text of the document refers to the confederates in the third person plural, and only one single sentence uses "we." This is the so-called judges clause in which the treaty partners unanimously swear that they will accept no judge who is not a native of the valleys or who has come by his office through bribery. By including this clause in the treaty, the forest cantons show their deep objection to any henchmen of a foreign power. The treaty emphasises their basic political principle: they are determined to be masters in their own house. They have had enough of alien administrators.

II TELL—FACT OR FICTION?

The 13th century offers no documentary proof of a popular uprising. The confederates had, in fact, no historian whose work has come down to us; and not until the 15th century was there a published account of the events surrounding the Everlasting Alliance. It was provided in the *White Book of Sarnen*, which appeared in 1470. The

---

* Nidwalden and Obwalden merged as Unterwalden but later again followed separate paths in various respects.

story, perhaps based on earlier chronicles which have disappeared, was subsequently included in the *Chronicon Helveticum* of the 16th century historian Aegidius Tschudi and in Johannes von Müller's *History of the Swiss Confederation* of 1786. It entered world literature with the publication in 1804 of Schiller's drama *Wilhelm Tell*.

Is the famous story of Tell and the uprising against tyranny fact or fiction, or perhaps a mixture of both? Certainly, its dramatic force is simple and persuasive. On the one side we have the local officials, abusing their power, exploiting the people of the valleys, and ignoring hard-won liberties. On the other side, there are the people's representatives, swearing to put a stop to tyranny and organising their conspiracy at a secret meeting in the Rütli, a meadow bordering Lake Lucerne. The symbol of tyranny is the bailiff Gessler, the *Vogt* in Uri. The symbol of revolt is Tell, who refuses to obey the order to salute Gessler's hat displayed on a staff at Altdorf. The punishment Tell faces for this refusal is an unnerving test of his courage. But in successfully shooting the apple from his son's head, he triumphs over Gessler; and in killing him for his cruelty, he sets the torch to the popular uprising which brings the castles of the oppressors crashing down in flames.

Sceptical historians long relegated all this to the realm of fable, and were unreceptive even to the heart of the matter. But some details of the narrative, once dismissed as ridiculous, are now known to have a firm historical foundation. The hat on the staff was in fact a medieval symbol of jurisdiction. The castles burned in the uprising are shown by excavations to have been reduced to ruins at that time. We now also know that the confederate leader, Rudolf Stauffacher, owned a house built of stone, despite the Habsburg monopoly of stone buildings, and thus confronted men like Gessler with a permanent challenge to their pretensions of authority. Quite possibly various details were added to embellish the story by narrators who also introduced foreign legends into Switzerland. Thus part of the exchange between Gessler and Tell is word for word the same as in the Nordic tale of Toko the marksman, written down by a Dane about 1200. But whatever the historical truth of the circumstances surrounding the origin of the Confederation, the features of the story which the Swiss themselves consider vital point to a deeply ingrained principle: the key to the confederate system has always been co-operation between individual

and community. Tell represents the strong enterprising individual who
is most powerful on his own; but the people who concluded the Everlasting Alliance in the Rütli became strong through unity. Tell's courage was needed to provide the impetus, but it was for the confederates
to exploit the situation. It was not enough, however, to destroy the
castles and drive out the *Vögte*. The people had to make sure that
the enemy they had expelled did not return with armed support to
restore his position.

III   THE BATTLE OF MORGARTEN

The forest communities were not the only ones who feared the power
of the Habsburgs. Zürich, which as an imperial city was directly
subordinate only to the crown, also considered itself threatened; and
as a result it concluded an alliance with Uri and Schwyz. Nevertheless,
it looked as though this anti-Habsburg front would not be a match
for the forces at the command of Albert, King Rudolf's son. His
troops defeated Zürich and a campaign against the cantons seemed
imminent; but then the complex contest for the imperial crown
brought them temporary relief in another period of growing instability
for the Empire. First, in 1292 the electoral princes chose as Rudolf's
successor not Albert of Habsburg but the Rhenish Count Adolf of
Nassau. Within six years, however, Adolf was unable to hold his own
against his rival and lost both the imperial crown and his life in battle.
After this, the electors had no option but to appoint the victorious
Albert. Yet his greed to extend his dynastic power ultimately led to
his downfall, and in 1308 he was murdered by a member of his own
family near the ancestral castle in the Aargau.

As Albert's sons were still too young for the crown, the way was
open for the electors to confer it on a contender from another dynasty
—Henry, Count of Luxembourg. Henry not only confirmed the privileges of Uri and Schwyz, which had given them direct and exclusive
dependence on the crown, but he also granted the same status to
Unterwalden. On Henry's death within the fifth year of his reign,
however, the sons of Albert of Habsburg put forward their claims to
the throne. The electoral princes were divided: only half of them
chose the Habsburg contender Frederick the Fair, while the others
selected Lewis, duke of Bavaria. The dispute led to a war of succession

in Germany, at the end of which the Habsburg drive to gain the imperial throne was thwarted for more than a century.

In the struggle, the forest cantons supported the opponents of the Habsburgs; and as a reprisal for this, Frederick's brother Duke Leopold planned a triple assault on central Switzerland—via the Brünig pass, across the lake from Lucerne, and along the shore of Lake Zug. The aim was to force the confederates to their knees, particularly Schwyz which was contesting the abbey of Einsiedeln that stood under Habsburg protection. The forest cantons had made their preparations: where there were gaps in the natural ring of mountains they barred the attackers' way with dry-stone walls—*Letzi*—and other fortifications. Only at the Morgarten pass was a breach left open—and that was a trap. When Duke Leopold with 2,000 mounted knights, clad in heavy armour, rode along the track at the edge of Lake Aegeri on 15 November 1315, the defenders were waiting to pounce. They hurled rocks and tree trunks down on the knights, and then descended on them with the favourite weapon of the confederates—the halberd with its head of axe and spike. The knights were driven into the lake and swamp, and three-quarters of them perished. The Swiss foot soldiers had triumphed over the glittering cavalry of Habsburg. The ripples of the victory went far beyond Lake Aegeri; and although Leopold himself survived the battle, it was said afterwards in Switzerland that "mounted knights were much thinner on the ground."

The Habsburg attempt to wage economic war was equally unsuccessful. It is true that the valleys were poor in natural resources, and depended for much of their supply of corn, salt and iron on imports, which could be interrupted by a blockade of the Gotthard route. But the confederates were willing to go short of food rather than sacrifice their freedom. They followed up their sensational military victory at Morgarten by strengthening their alliance and then enlarging it. At Brunnen, on 9 December 1315, Uri, Schwyz and Unterwalden drew up a new document and affirmed, this time in robust German, that thenceforth no member of the Confederation was to make peace or treaties without the advice and consent of the others; and no member was even to parley with outsiders, unless all the others were told. United at home, the three communities were resolved in future to conduct a fully co-ordinated external policy.

It was not long before they won support from the port and market town of Lucerne. The Morgarten war with the diversion of the Gotthard traffic had greatly harmed the economy of the town, which was an important strategic link both on the north-south trade routes and in the Habsburg military drive against the forest cantons. Public opinion in Lucerne, which was still a Habsburg possession, moved in favour of the confederates, the more so since Habsburg officials hampered the town's advance towards autonomy under its own burgomaster and council and sought to diminish its liberties. In 1332 the mood had changed sufficiently for Lucerne to join the Confederation. It was an alliance between town and country, co-operating on a basis of equality. It did not result in the town controlling the rural population because the forest cantons had already completed their great political advance in forging the Confederation before Lucerne requested their popular assemblies to be admitted as a member.

So within 17 years of Morgarten, the Confederation had been strengthened for the first time. The ring of allies around Lake Lucerne was complete; their vital lines of communication were secured. The Habsburgs had been out-manoeuvred.

IV THE LANDSGEMEINDEN AND THE TOWNS

The Treaty of Alliance of 1291 contains many principles which are still of relevance today. But the democratic roots of the Swiss state lie not so much in the document itself as in the people it brought together. The treaty does not mention a single individual by name. It was the community of each valley as a whole which took the oath and set its seal on the alliance. The provisions of the treaty were debated and approved at each community's popular assembly, the *Landsgemeinde,* which in its essential features was a model of the purest democracy.

The *Landsgemeinde,* which still exists in Obwalden, Nidwalden, Appenzell and Glarus, springs from two sources. One lies in the old Germanic public assembly, which acted as a court of justice and was attended by free men carrying their swords, just as to this day the men of Appenzell come to the *Landsgemeinde* with swords or bayonets. The other root is economic, and derives from the way the Alemanni administered the *Allmende,* the area of land which remained in joint occupation by the community. The common use of forests and mountain pastures was the subject of debate, concessions and agreement in the early agricultural communities, while another matter of common concern was the preservation of forests to act as a defence against avalanches. Raw materials such as ores and salt were presumably imported jointly, or at least the price and distribution were settled collectively. "One for all and all for one" was an established economic fact before it became a battle-cry; and it was in the agricultural community that the medieval peasant saw social equality in practice. Collaboration between private peasants on their own farmsteads and within the community in other matters gave protection to the weak without strangling the enterprising. The meetings at which questions of common property were debated were forerunners of democratic government. Since the Alpine farmers often had to travel fairly long distances to attend them it was decided to arrange for economic affairs and jurisdiction to be dealt with on the same day at the same place. This lent the meetings a constitutional character.

The significance of the *Landsgemeinde* for Switzerland's democratic evolution cannot be overrated. The people assembled in the open air on common land, standing in a great circle as is still the practice in Glarus, and raising their arms to the sky to take the oath. Every member had the right to submit proposals and take part in the debate. The majority decided and the minority accepted its verdict. The people elected the *Landamman,* who exercised low justice over the community and was the most senior of several *Ammänner* with similar functions. His authority and position depended wholly on the confidence of the people, who called him to the centre of the circle and bestowed on him the sword and seals of office. No emperor could sustain him against the vote of his fellow citizens.

In the Alpine lands the third estate of the working people was reaching political maturity 500 years before the French Revolution proclaimed the equality of man. The aristocrat's vote weighed no more than that of the poorest peasant from the most remote valley. Nor did the clergy enjoy the privileges they had in other countries. The very earliest resolutions of the *Landsgemeinde* of Schwyz declared: "If monasteries in this land do not want to pay taxes and other dues according to their property as do other country people, they shall keep away from field, water, forest and pasture."

Switzerland's early democracy has often been misrepresented. But

the principles which illuminated the Confederation at its inception
remained alive for a later generation to reshape—guided by the ideals
of free self-government, equality and respect for human dignity.

*   *   *

The development of the Confederation was, of course, not only the
work of the Alpine peasantry. The people of the towns, too, made
their contribution to a system which replaced the relationship of overlord and subject by the more humane and dignified status of fellow
citizen. The tenacity of the peasants, with roots deep in their homeland, was admirably complemented by the enterprising spirit of
merchants and artisans whose business brought them into closer contact with the world beyond.

The Swiss towns developed at economically and strategically favourable spots, often on the sites of earlier large Roman settlements. Frequently, they were dependent on local aristocrats or the Church:
Berne and Fribourg, for example, were both founded as military posts
in the 12th century by the Counts of Zähringen. The expansion of
trade and craft specialisation brought growing knowledge and skill
and engendered a freer way of thinking. The people found oppression
by powerful overlords more and more unbearable. Bondsmen migrated
to the towns, and unless their masters reclaimed them within a year
they were regarded as free men. As their populations grew, the towns
demanded greater independence. Under the leadership of their elected
councils, the citizens steadily increased their rights and privileges until
they attained complete self-government. The supreme aim of a medieval town was the status of a free imperial city under the direct protection of the Emperor.

Each town chose its own road to freedom. In Zürich matters took
a remarkable turn. The oligarchy of knights, merchants and traders
had grown rich from the manufacture of silk and considered they had
a right to run affairs in their own way. But they were compelled to
share control in the government by the ambitious Rudolf Brun, a
member of the upper class who assumed leadership of the craft guilds
and thus won for himself great personal power. From then on 13 guild-
masters sat on the town council facing 13 representatives of the nobility and merchants. In days to come there was a Great Council of
200 which supervised the executive. The council comprised about one-

The heart of the country and its history: Lake Lucerne, the *Vierwaldstättersee*, seen in this view from Mount Pilatus, looking towards the mountains of central Switzerland.

The living tradition of Swiss political life: the
Landsgemeinde meets in Glarus. Such
assemblies of the people are rooted deep in
the history of Switzerland and are the basis of
its democracy.

fifth of the citizens, ensuring that the final decisions lay, if not with the whole community as in the case of the *Landsgemeinde,* then at least with a large number of its representatives. Each of the craft guilds was itself a nucleus of democracy. Spreading up the Rhine, the guilds' movement was making an important impact on the political life of the towns of northern Switzerland, producing a kind of planned economy under state protection, with trades, professions, and quality of products legally prescribed and controlled. Handicrafts flourished and a vigorous middle class came into being whose members jealously guarded their high reputation as craftsmen.

The trades unionist tendencies among the townspeople soon clashed with the traditional feudal attitudes of the nobility and the princes of the Church. In this tense situation the towns cast about for allies. City leagues were founded, but most of them were broken up by the massive strength of the knights. The alliances with the confederates proved more dependable. When Rudolf Brun, by then elected Zürich's burgomaster for life, realised that the Habsburgs were backing the defeated nobles and merchants and supporting their plots to regain control of the town council, he turned for help to Habsburg's most bitter opponents. In 1351, Zürich made a perpetual pact with the forest cantons and Lucerne. This provided for mutual assistance within a large area which included important passes in the Gotthard region.

Berne, too, knew the value of armed assistance from the confederates. A tradition of temporary alliances with them dating back many decades proved useful when the city's territorial ambitions were challenged by the town of Fribourg and the feudal armies of neighbouring areas, with the encouragement of the Habsburgs. Berne called on the forest cantons for help. In the crucial battle at Laupen in the summer of 1339 confederate troops held the mounted knights in check until Berne's commander, Rudolf von Erlach, had defeated the enemy foot soldiers. In 1353 the comrades-in-arms of Laupen became confederates in the Everlasting Alliance which thus gained an important outpost in the west.

Meanwhile the expanding Confederation had also acquired new pillars in the east and the north with the accession of two of Schwyz's outlying neighbours. At the beginning of June 1352, the community of Glarus was incorporated; and the Habsburg township and region of Zug were admitted at the end of the same month. These treaties came into full force only after a series of setbacks. For the members of the alliance, now numbering eight, had to assert and uphold their liberty and the novel concept of confederation in a long and grim struggle against opponents who stood for an entirely different social and political order.

3

From Freedom to Power

I THE PEOPLE'S ARMY

THE YEARS from 1386 to 1515 were the most turbulent in Swiss history. The period began with another victory over the Habsburgs and ended in a retreat from a foreign battlefield which marked the beginnings of the country's policy of neutrality. In the years between, the Confederation seldom knew real peace for long in its struggle to rally more support, secure its borders and win external recognition. It fought wars involving all its powerful neighbours, and showed that it too could be a power in Europe, with a force of fighting men who were feared, admired and then courted as mercenaries. At the same time, the Confederation was rent by civil war in which the divisions between town and country that were long to bedevil it first became acute. From this period of war and internal strife, the nation took shape; its future course was set in the 130 years of triumph and adversity that started towards the end of the 14th century with renewed struggle against the Habsburgs.

By that time the knights, so vain about their battle honours, seem to have recovered from that unfortunate affair of 1315, their crushing defeat at Morgarten. As professional soldiers, they still affected to sneer at the peasants and artisans who managed to wield a halberd as skilfully as a pitchfork or hammer, and by 1386 they felt the time had come to restore their shaken prestige. The opportunity they could not ignore was a defiant move by Lucerne to throw off what was left of Habsburg control and to expand its territory by imposing citizenship on the nearby Habsburg town of Sempach. Duke Leopold III, lauded in his day as the flower of knighthood, took up the challenge and confidently laid siege to Sempach. Meanwhile, nobles from many parts of Europe converged to settle accounts with the peasant confederates who rallied to Lucerne's support.

When the battle began in July 1386, Leopold was determined not to allow the Swiss foot-soldiers to outwit the Habsburg cavalry as they had done at Morgarten. He therefore ordered his men-at-arms to dismount and advance on a broad front. They surged forward with their long lances against the shorter swords and halberds of their opponents, threatening to outflank, encircle and then impale them. But the plan turned out to be ill-conceived. The confederates fought back at close quarters, Leopold was killed and his forces were routed. The battle gave the Swiss not only a victory but a hero whose exploits have become legendary, Arnold von Winkelried. The story is that he closed with the enemy, tore aside their lances, and opened up a gap in their line of advance, so enabling his comrades to make the best use of their mobility and shorter weapons as they poured through the breach and hacked the broken enemy line to pieces. But whatever the details, the outcome is undisputed : the Swiss, in their second big battle with the Habsburgs, had triumphed again.

They did not at once exploit their victory. Another seven years passed before the eight confederate communities, as well as the town of Solothurn in the north-west, agreed on terms for military co-operation in the *Sempacherbrief,* the Covenant of Sempach of 1393. The delay gave the Habsburgs the opportunity to try their luck once more. This time they attempted to reconquer Glarus, the territory to the east of Schwyz which had first joined the Confederation in 1352. When the Habsburg forces attacked in the early spring of 1388, everything seemed to be in their favour. The men of Glarus were vastly outnumbered and could not rely on help from across the snow-covered mountains. But the battle at Näfels produced another surprise : the knights were soundly beaten yet again.

Another chapter in the expansion of the Confederation was written by the people of Appenzell in the north-east and the monastery of St. Gallen. In the days of Rudolf of Habsburg, the town of St. Gallen was ruled by an ambitious abbot, Berchtold von Falkenstein, whose system of administration and the taxes he imposed left both the townspeople and the Appenzell peasantry ready for rebellion. When he died, the people danced in the streets and vowed to protect themselves against exploitation in the future. To this end, they entered into an alliance with the League of Swabian Towns which was formed in 1376 to present a united front against the nobility. Their trust in the

League was shown to be misplaced, however, when it left them in the lurch, and even supported an Austrian campaign against Appenzell. In 1405, the Austrians attempted to storm the Appenzell highlands, but were driven back to the Rhine valley. Later, Appenzell was supported by the citizens of St. Gallen in an offensive against Austria as far as the Arlberg; but their union was over-extended and neither solid nor strong enough to withstand the counterblow to come. When its forces reached Bregenz on the east bank of Lake Constance, they met defeat and their alliance was broken. The nobles were set on revenge; but Appenzell clung to its new freedom and became an ally of the Confederation, which offered more reliable support than the Swabian League as well as the reputation of being well able to defend itself.

The military victories for which the confederates had become renowned were not due merely to favourable circumstances. The nobles had failed to appreciate the toughness of their opponents. Their pluck and stamina came from the hard conditions of Alpine life, and made them a formidable and experienced band of fighters who, whenever possible, chose a mountainous terrain where their speed and mobility put the armoured knights at a disadvantage. The confederates knew they were fighting for their homes and the freedom of their country. They went into battle not on the orders of an overlord but by the decision of the popular assembly. A people's army was a matter of course, including in its ranks all men over 18 and sometimes even 14-year-old boys. If necessary, everyone joined the fight.

II   CIVIL WAR

A free and united Confederation was the goal; but in the struggle to achieve it, the towns and cantons passed through a number of internal crises. The first arose from a dispute which Zürich had with Schwyz and finally with the rest of the confederates. Its cause was the Toggenburg inheritance, to which there were several claimants, and its outcome was the country's first civil war.

The last of the Toggenburgs, Count Frederick VII, had amassed extensive possessions in an area of eastern Switzerland stretching from the river Thur to the glaciers of the Silvretta and controlling routes by river and lake which were vital for moving bulk cargo. Zürich was eager to dominate the route to the Walensee via the valley of the Linth and also the approaches to the Alpine passes. But Schwyz too had its eye on the Linth valley, because only in that north-easterly direction could it expand beyond its borders. Each of the rivals made a point of currying favour with Count Frederick of Toggenburg, but when he died childless in 1436, he left no clear testament about his possessions. Some accounts suggest this was a piece of calculated malice designed to cause trouble between the peasants of Schwyz and the townspeople of Zürich. If this is true, the rivals certainly carried out Frederick's intentions.

In the contest that followed, each side was led by an outstanding man of the time—Schwyz by its *Landamman,* chief magistrate Ital Reding, and Zürich by its burgomaster, Rudolf Stüssi. Events were to show that the wily Reding and his rural followers were more than a match for the townsmen under the inflexible Stüssi. Zürich sought help from its arch enemies, the Habsburgs, who were finally securing an enduring hold on the imperial crown after an interval of more than a century. In these circumstances, there was a danger of the Habsburg Emperor exploiting strife in Switzerland to regain ancient possessions and totally destroy the divided Confederation. Aware of this threat, its other members threw in their lot with Schwyz against Zürich.

In 1443, the confederates inflicted a decisive defeat on a combined force of Zürich and Austria not far from the city's walls, at St. Jakob on the river Sihl; and burgomaster Stüssi was killed in the fighting. The way was now open for a campaign against Zürich. Its last outpost, the little town of Greifensee, fell to the onslaught and the defenders were shown no mercy : all of them, apart from a few old men and boys, were executed. A confederate force then laid siege to Zürich; but the citizens were soon encouraged by news that heralded unexpected relief.

At this time the Habsburg Emperor was on good terms with Charles VII of France, and called on him to help Austria and Zürich. Since France had just concluded a truce with England, virtually ending the Hundred Years War, large numbers of French mercenaries were without a fight on their hands and were causing nothing but trouble in France. Charles VII was therefore glad to get rid of these Armagnacs, as they were known, by sending 30,000 of them to Switzerland. Their first encounter was with a Swiss advance guard of a mere 1,500 men. This small contingent, encouraged by a few successful skirmishes, rashly crossed the river Birs to press home an attack. In doing so, the troops ignored orders and invited disaster, but their courage was never to be forgotten.

At St. Jakob an der Birs, on 26 August 1444, they waged the most heroic battle in Swiss history. Outnumbered 20 to 1, they astounded the enemy by their bravery and fought to the last man rather than surrender. Their courageous stand left a deep impression on the French, who at that time knew little about Swiss fighting qualities; and military defeat was turned into political victory. For the Dauphin, the future King Louis XI of France, who was in nominal command of the Armagnacs, refused to let his forces advance into confederate territory. Instead, he put out peace feelers and even sought to enlist Swiss soldiers in the service of France, the first of a long line of French rulers to do so. His attitude decided the outcome of the civil war. Warships which Austria had built for use on Lake Zürich failed to turn the scales and Austrian troops who crossed the Rhine at Ragaz in 1446 were defeated by the confederates.

Peace was finally concluded in 1450, when Zürich agreed to renounce its pact with Austria and was once again accepted into the Confederation. The civil war which might have destroyed it in fact left the Confederation stronger than before. From now on it began to take its name from the canton which produced the heroes of St. Jakob an der Birs. Schwyz was the heart of Switzerland; and the white cross in the corner of the red standard of Schwyz was later brought to the centre of the national flag of Switzerland.

III FURTHER EXPANSION

The confederates had long realised that to retain their freedom it was important to control the approaches to their territory. In the north, the principal routes converged in Aargau, south of the Rhine between Berne and Zürich. It was here that the Habsburgs had their ancestral castle; and they still dominated strong-points along the river Aare, such as Aarburg and Brugg, which they could use as a springboard for a campaign of reconquest. Apart from these strategic considerations there were economic factors involved, for the area where the rivers Aare, Limmat and Reuss flow together was a rich granary.

Early in the 15th century, the prevailing conditions favoured a Swiss move to take over these Habsburg possessions. The Church was rent by the great schism, with three Popes claiming the Holy See. In 1414, as confusion continued, hundreds of princes of the Church came together at the Council of Constance in an effort to heal their divisions. The corrupt Pope who had taken the title John XXIII arrived at Lake Constance in an effort to cling to power; and when the Council passed him over, he turned for help to his supporter Frederick of Austria. It was this situation that gave the Confederation its opportunity. For the Emperor Sigismund of Bohemia was deeply angered by Frederick's attitude, put him under the imperial ban and urged the Swiss to move against the Austrian lands.

Even the people of Berne, who had the reputation of being a little slow, were stirred by this prospect of conquest, with the chance it offered of rounding off confederate territory and chasing the Austrians from the region south of the Jura. The Bernese advanced as far as Brugg, while forces from Zürich, Lucerne and the other cantons overran areas elsewhere in Aargau, including the town of Baden in the north and the Freiamt in the south. When the occupation was complete, the cantons agreed on a system of joint rule in the interests of them all. This establishment of common lordship (*gemeine Herrschaft*) opened a new stage in their co-operation, forging closer links which strengthened their sense of union. In one way, however, the situation meant a betrayal of their original ideals which, in time, they would have cause to regret. The Confederation had come into being because the people detested the rule of alien *Vögte*. Now they were imposing it on others.

In the drive to achieve security in the outlying territories, attention now switched to the neighbouring Italians. Just as in the north the Habsburgs had been entrenched in Aargau, so in the south the Visconti family of Milan had seized control of the approaches to the central Alps. The two ambitious dynasties were related, and in the Sempach campaign the Swiss had sensed the danger of a war on two fronts since the Visconti not only sent troops to help the Austrians, but also blocked the Gotthard route near the heavily-fortified town of Bellinzona. It was therefore essential in the interests of Switzerland's defence to command this gateway to Italy and the mountain passes. Economic factors also again played a part, as they had done in the north. For the route was vital to the Swiss mountain peasants who used it to drive their animals to market in Italy. The people of Uri, therefore, made a determined attempt to occupy the southern slopes of the Gotthard pass. After a daring campaign in the mountain valleys of the Ticino, however, the confederates were defeated at Arbedo, just north of Bellinzona, in 1422. The people of Uri were more concerned about the outcome than the others, because to them the Gotthard artery was a matter of economic life and death; and 17 years later, in another campaign south of the pass, they occupied the Valle Leventina, bringing it once and for all under Swiss rule.

For some years after this, the external growth of the Confederation was interrupted by the civil war with Zürich. But when the confederates were reunited, their prestige began to rise. Several towns and monasteries looked to them for protection. The Abbot of St. Gallen was one who sought their friendship : so did the towns of St. Gallen, Schaffhausen and Bienne. These towns became neither subjects nor equal members of the Confederation, but were given an intermediate status as allies—so-called *Zugewandte Orte*. In the Diet, the congress of representatives from the cantons, they were only permitted to take part in discussions which directly concerned them. In foreign policy matters, they were subject to the confederates' veto; and they owed a duty to join any armed campaigns undertaken by the Confederation in return for its military protection.

The significance of this arrangement was seen within the next few years, when the Austrians were driven out of their remaining strongholds in Thurgau, the area west of Lake Constance which divided the Confederation from its new allies Schaffhausen and St. Gallen. The occasion for this expansion, like the earlier advance in Aargau, was a dispute beyond the Confederation's borders, this time between Pope Pius II and Duke Sigismund of Austria. The Pope urged the confederates to occupy Thurgau. They for their part were not going to miss the opportunity such a "sacred war" gave them for achieving their ambition to secure the frontier on the Rhine. So in 1460, they swept into Thurgau, and continued their advance until the Austrians were left with hardly a stronghold south of the Rhine valley. The confederates decided to rule Thurgau in the same way as they did the

Aargau territories, establishing a common lordship, with joint collection of taxes and dues and with a *Vogt* making his appearance to supervise the administration.

A generation later, two more areas of strategic importance were brought under joint rule as common lordships, the Rheintal area—now part of the canton of St. Gallen—and Sargans. The town of Sargans was vital because it commanded two roads from the Alpine passes, one towards the Walensee and Zürich, the other towards Lake Constance and south Germany. Shared control of all these strategic frontier positions ensured that it would be in the interests of all the confederates to defend them jointly in time of war.

IV WAR AGAINST BURGUNDY

When the Swiss pushed their frontiers to the banks of the Rhine and Lake Constance, Europe began to take them seriously. Until then the major powers had regarded Switzerland's struggle for liberty as no more than an internal affair of concern to the Austrian rulers, and it was thought that the baffling military skill of the peasant soldiers was confined to the terrain they knew best, the Alps. But things looked different in 1468 when the confederates advanced northwards in response to a call for help from the imperial city of Mühlhausen on the Rhine. Mühlhausen was being threatened by the local nobility supported by Duke Sigismund of Austria; but the appearance of the Swiss forces put an end to this threat, and ensured that it remained a free city. During the campaign the castles of the nobles were burned and there was a good deal of looting. The Swiss troops, elated by their triumph, were in the mood for a further test of strength.

On their return march they made for the Rhine town of Waldshut, which was under Austrian control. For five weeks they laid siege to it; and in the end Austria bought them off by undertaking to pay them 10,000 gulden, regarding no price too high to prevent the establishment of a confederate bridgehead on the right bank of the Rhine. To get the money, the impecunious Duke Sigismund had to knock at the gates of Europe's richest treasury—Burgundy. Its ruler Charles the Bold, who was as shrewd as he was arrogant, immediately advanced him five times the amount. But this was no act of class loyalty. Charles had quite different motives. He was sure Sigismund was not in a position to repay the money; and if it was not forthcoming, he hoped to acquire all Sigismund's rights in Upper Alsace and in four Rhine towns, including Waldshut, as well as other Austrian privileges in the area. Charles coveted this territory as a link between his northern possessions, Brabant and Flanders, and his southern ones, reaching from the Jura to the river Loire. Its acquisition would have been a glorious conclusion to 100 years of Burgundian expansion.

The ambition and power of Burgundy worried both the Emperor and Louis XI of France, but especially the latter. The Austrian Duke also realised he was in a perilous situation as a result of his deal with Charles, who was already having the pledged territories governed as his own through a ruthless nobleman, Peter von Hagenbach. The time had come for the astute king of France to act, and his first step was to encourage all who had a grievance against Charles to sink their differences and rally in an anti-Burgundy front. It was of supreme importance to him to bring about a reconciliation between Austria and the confederates, whose gallantry he had personally experienced in the battle of St. Jakob an der Birs. In 1474, Sigismund and most of the cantons reached an agreement: he unreservedly recognised the Confederation, which in turn promised to help Austria in regaining the pledged territories. But when the money for this was made available, Charles refused to accept it. The local people thereupon arrested, tried and executed his unpopular *Vogt* Hagenbach in the presence of Swiss emissaries.

Charles was bound to react to the challenge. Yet when the clash came in 1476, the confederates were abandoned by both the French king and the Emperor. The fortress of Grandson, by Lake Neuchâtel, was captured by Charles' army; and the men of the garrison, who pleaded in vain for mercy, were drowned in the lake or hanged. Had they been able to stand their ground for another two or three days till a Swiss relieving force arrived, they would have shared in a great victory—and one unparalleled in the country's history for the fabulous booty it yielded. In the battle of Grandson, the Burgundians learned what an effective power the Swiss forces had become; but though defeated, Charles' army was not destroyed, and it was soon ready to renew the fight.

In June 1476 Charles appeared with 20,000 men at the walled town of Morat between Lake Neuchâtel and Berne. Morat was

defended by a Bernese garrison under Adrian von Bubenberg, who set
his face against surrender and held out until reinforcements could
arrive. Among them was a contingent from Zürich, led by the man
who was to become celebrated as the city's burgomaster, Hans Waldmann. They covered the 80 miles to Berne in a forced march of two
and a half days, and then pressed on to Morat. The day after their
arrival brought victory to the confederates. This time the Burgundian
army was virtually destroyed : its disastrous casualties included 10,000
men killed. Charles the Bold's campaign had come to nothing, and
six months later he was dead. His mutilated body was found near a
frozen pond not far from the town of Nancy in Lorraine. Before he
died he had lost his last battle, beaten by a former ally, René of Lorraine, and a hired force of Swiss under Waldmann. The power of
Burgundy was broken. Louis XI had achieved what he wanted; and
the Habsburgs, too, could be content. But what of the Swiss, who had
borne the brunt of the fighting?

V   Town versus Country

The defeat of Burgundy turned out to be a mixed blessing for the
confederates. They had beaten off the attack from the west, and come
through to victory on their borders. They had proved themselves at
least the equals of any soldiers in Europe. But when it came to securing the true benefits of victory, battle honours were no match for the
sly diplomacy of Louis XI, who was determined that France should
be the chief beneficiary of the eclipse of Burgundy.

The Swiss indeed received a big financial share in the spoils; and
Berne in particular was left in a powerful position as a result of the
war. But all this seemed to distort the values and ideals of the people.
It was as though the tale of the peasant who suddenly found himself
wearing princely gowns and jewels had come true for a whole nation.
The victors of Grandson were strutting about in silk and velvet,
and they seemed to be turning into arrogant little tyrants. Along with
their coarse shirts, they had also discarded the will to face the harsh
realities of the situation. As soon as external pressure was removed,
the internal jealousies engendered by prosperity and victory came to
the surface, in particular the rivalry between town and country. The

spoils of war—the rich stocks of weapons and jewels which Burgundy had yielded—were the chief cause of the divisions. How was this booty to be distributed? The cities wanted it done on the basis of population, which would have been to their advantage. The country cantons insisted that this method would be unfair to them—although in fact the cities had provided many more troops for the war.

Before long the peasants of central Switzerland were marching westwards, this time to stake their claim to the booty of war and to demand ransoms to which they felt entitled in Geneva and Savoy. Ahead of them went a provocative banner, displaying a picture of a sow. A demonstration like this alarmed prosperous Berne and Lucerne, especially as they feared it would inflame rebellion among the peasants who had become their subjects in increasing numbers. The towns of Solothurn and Fribourg had similar anxieties; and the constitutional position of these two magnified the divisions between town and country. They had been comrades-in-arms of the Confederation during the war against Burgundy, and they now felt the time had come to apply for membership of the Confederation. Their application was supported by the cities, but opposed by the country cantons who feared that it would only add to the power of the urban areas.

A gulf had opened between town and country right across the Confederation, and another civil war threatened. At this point, a strange figure emerges: the hermit Niklaus von Flüe, known as Brother Klaus, a man of piety and of great authority among the people. He remains to us an enigmatic character; but it is clear that his intervention averted the worst dangers to the country. Accepting his counsel, the eight cantons met at the Diet of Stans on 22 December 1481, and drew up an historic covenant—the *Stanser Verkommnis*—resolving matters which had been dividing them. It outlined a compromise for distributing the spoils of war. It did justice to Fribourg's and Solothurn's claims to membership of the Confederation. And to keep the spirit of union alive among the confederates it laid down that every five years they would reaffirm two of their previous agreements: the Covenant of Sempach of 1393, which had defined their military co-operation, and the Priests' Charter of 1370, which had curtailed the privileges of the clergy.

The *Stanser Verkommnis,* which pulled the Confederation together

at its moment of great internal danger, was a tribute to the influence
of the mystic, Brother Klaus, who had exchanged possessions, position and family for poverty and the reflective life. In Zürich at that
time, another man who played a great part in these eventful years
was rising to power and affluence; this was Hans Waldmann, who
had shared in the battle honours at Morat. Now burgomaster of
Zürich, he was known as the richest man in the Confederation, and
his influence stretched beyond its borders. He had acquired this
position through a mixture of great military ability and political
adroitness, as well as by the favours of princes. Potentially it was a
position offering great scope for benefiting Zürich and the Confederation. Waldmann could perhaps have achieved great things. Instead,
he became an intolerable dictator. The ostentation of his private life
was the more offensive since he issued a stringent code of ethics for
his fellow citizens. Charges of bribery were levelled at him; but still
the dictatorial measures flowed. Finally, the peasants rebelled. They
enlisted support among the citizens; and the other confederates did
nothing to stop Waldmann's overthrow. In 1489, he was arrested,
condemned and executed.

VI   THE SWABIAN WAR AND THE MILANESE CAMPAIGNS

It had not been the intention of the founders of the Confederation to
break all ties with the Empire. On the contrary, they had always
been eager to have their privileges confirmed by each successive
Emperor. Their objection had only been to upstart officials who tried
to lord it over them. But the situation had now changed : from accepting the purely nominal direct supremacy of a distant ruler, they had
become alienated from the Empire. Their attitude grew into hostility
when the Habsburg Emperor sided with Zürich during the civil war,
and when in the Burgundian war he did nothing to protect the Swiss
garrison at Grandson from massacre. The confederates therefore had
the greatest misgivings when a new Habsburg Emperor, Maximilian
I, announced his plans for imperial reforms. He intended to establish
an Imperial Supreme Court (*Reichskammergericht*) as a final court of
appeal, and to introduce a general tax throughout the Empire. The
Swiss bitterly resented this attempt to force them to give up their own

well-tried Germanic laws in favour of an innovation based on Roman concepts. And they were determined to resist.

In the Swabian war, which broke out in January 1499, Maximilian had on his side the Swabian League, the group of South German towns which was opposing any further Swiss expansion. Facing them were the eastern Swiss communities who over the years had formed their own leagues to defend their independence. There were three of these: the *Gotteshausbund*—the League of God's House formed around Chur; the *Graue Bund*—the Grey League at Ilanz on the upper Rhine; and the *Zehngerichtebund*—the Ten Jurisdictions League at Davos. The three groups were united by a passion for liberty which transcended the geographical obstacles and linguistic differences among them. Two of the leagues were, in fact, tri-lingual; and this area of the Grisons can justly be described as the testing ground of linguistic harmony in Switzerland.

When war began, the leagues of the Grisons were not alone: shortly beforehand, two of them had formed a perpetual alliance with the confederates. The fighting started after an attack by imperial forces on the ancient monastery of Müstair in the Münstertal, and before long the people of the Grisons and their confederate neighbours were involved in a great struggle against the German-Austrian enemy. In the nine months that war lasted, there was a series of fierce battles over a 300-mile long front, and in fighting on the river Calven the Grisons lost their inspiring leader, Fontana. But they and their allies finally emerged victorious. After a decisive Swiss success at Dornach near Basle, Maximilian was compelled to give up the struggle.

The Peace of Basle of September 1499 made no mention of the imperial reforms Maximilian had intended to impose. In fact, if not yet in name, Switzerland was now independent of the Empire, though legal independence still had to wait one-and-a-half centuries till the Peace of Westphalia of 1648. The Swiss victors had not extended their territory but had greatly enhanced their prestige. Schaffhausen and Basle both joined the Confederation as full members in 1501; and in 1513 the old ally, Appenzell, followed suit. Now the Confederation comprised 13 cantons, whose united power was recognised everywhere. The 13, brought together by more than two centuries of struggle against Habsburgs and Empire, were: the rural members Uri, Schwyz, Unterwalden, Zug, Glarus and Appenzell; and the cities and towns of Berne, Lucerne, Zürich, Fribourg, Solothurn, Basle and Schaffhausen.

*   *   *

After the Swabian war and the string of successes that preceded it, the military reputation of the Swiss stood so high that the great rulers of Europe competed for their services as soldiers. They had proved themselves formidable fighters; they knew there were rich rewards to be gained; and for many of them, war service was the only way to make a good living. They offered themselves to the bidders who promised the highest rewards; and it was as mercenaries that they became deeply involved in the struggle for the Duchy of Milan. The Duchy embraced areas to the south of the Alps which were of considerable economic importance both to the Swiss and others. It was of crucial value to the Empire as a key point on the trade route to the south; to the French with their territorial aspirations in Italy; and to the Pope in his concern to safeguard his own independence.

When the Duchy was faced with French invasion at the end of the 15th century, its ruler, Duke Ludovico, appealed to his brother-in-law, Emperor Maximilian, to call off the campaign against the confederates because he desperately needed their services as mercenaries. The Duke is said to have spent money like water to hire Swiss recruits. But Louis XII of France knew that they would fight for him as well if he offered the right price. So in 1500, the disastrous situation arose of Swiss facing Swiss under opposing foreign colours at the frontier town of Novara. The Diet urged them not to give battle; and a minority of those serving the Duke of Milan chose to desert him and accept a French promise of free retreat rather than fight their fellow countrymen. Betrayed by one of his mercenaries, the Duke was killed as he tried to escape. This "treachery of Novara" so deeply worried the confederates that a Diet at Baden in 1503 ruled that individual cantons must not conclude their own agreements for mercenary service with foreign powers.

This decision proved ineffective, however, partly because men were still attracted by the rich rewards involved and partly for the economic reason that the country could not feed all its people. It was in any event tempting for the confederates to think that they were in a position to wage war in their own interests and pursue a big-power policy. Would not conquest in northern Italy mean a solution to the population problem in Switzerland? The Alpine farming communities certainly had good reasons for supporting the drive to the south, for the Milanese territories offered an excellent market and a solution to the hard struggle for existence.

Prominent among the Alpine Swiss was Matthäus Schiner, once a goatherd but by the age of 34 Bishop of Sion. Schiner was a patriot with a burning hatred of France: it was therefore understandable that he should attract the attention of Pope Julius II, who was resolved to free Italy from what he regarded as the French barbarians. Schiner was made a cardinal as a reward for his success in arousing enthusiasm for this plan among his fellow-countrymen; and before long he had won the Emperor's support for it too. Until the Swiss joined in, the anti-French military alliance of the Holy League was not very effective, as the year 1512 was to show. In the spring, the League's forces were routed at Ravenna, and a French march on Rome seemed certain to follow. Then came the news that 18,000 Swiss soldiers had crossed the Alps into Lombardy and were rolling back the French front. The Pope hailed them as liberators of the Church, and bestowed a Papal flag of rich damask on each confederate community in recognition of their achievement. But the conquerors were after more than just fine words, Papal tributes or even gold. They sought territorial gains and they got them. The Grisons retained the Valtellina, Bormio and Chiavenna; common lordships were organised in the Valle Maggia, Lugano, Locarno and Mendrisio; and it was from Swiss hands that Maximilian Sforza, the son of Duke Ludovico, received the keys to his city of Milan—a gesture that virtually made Lombardy a protectorate of the Confederation.

The question was: could the Swiss keep and consolidate their gains? At first this seemed possible. In 1513, they faced another French attempt to conquer Lombardy. In a battle at Novara, the confederate foot soldiers overwhelmed the French artillery, and the Duchy of Milan was again freed. A few weeks later, a large Swiss army took the offensive on another front, crossing the Jura into France and marching on the town of Dijon. The commander of the French defenders, General Louis de la Trémouille, saved the town from being stormed only by agreeing that France would completely give up Lombardy and pay a huge sum to the Swiss. But the agreement was not worth the paper it was written on since Louis XII had not authorised it and did not consider himself bound by its terms.

When the young Francis I succeeded to the French throne in 1515, he vigorously resumed his predecessor's policy for the reconquest of Lombardy. With a force of 60,000 he crossed the Alps and won it back from a greatly weakened opponent. For the situation had changed in France's favour. The warrior Pope Julius II, who had been instrumental in forming the Holy League to drive the French out of Italy, had died and his place had been taken by the more peace-loving Leo X. In addition, the Swiss were now divided on their policies in Italy, many of them being unconcerned about the rights of Maximilian Sforza whom they had enthroned in Milan. Worst of all, bribes offered by France had paralysed their fighting spirit.

As a result, in September 1515 the men of Berne, Fribourg, Bienne and Solothurn were absent from the battlefield at Marignano. The remaining Swiss troops from Zürich and Zug were also considering withdrawal without a fight; but Cardinal Schiner, still in the vanguard of the campaign against France, persuaded them to attack the strongly fortified French positions. After two days of bitter fighting, during which they were heavily outnumbered, the confederates— hungry, cold and soaked to the skin—had to fall back on Milan. Then came a long, weary trek home. It was the beginning of Switzerland's retreat from big power politics altogether. The confederates retained what is today the canton of Ticino, but the Perpetual Peace of Fribourg in 1516 left them greatly overshadowed by France.

What was the cause of the Confederation's failure to take a place among the major powers? After playing for high stakes for several years, did it suddenly stop simply because it was a small country? Were the Alps an insuperable barrier to its advance towards the nearest sea? Did it lack military leaders of stature? Or was the decisive reason the mercenaries' inclination to succumb to foreign bribes? Possibly all these factors played a part. But the fundamental reason lay in the political structure of the Confederation. To develop as a great power it would have had to turn itself into a unitary state under some form of autocratic rule. This went right against the grain. A crucial choice had to be made, and the decision went in favour of freedom for each member of the Confederation. Because of this, the possibility of becoming a great military power was deliberately sacrificed. The defeat at Marignano signalled the birth of Swiss neutrality, the basis of future peace, freedom and unity. And at about the time of Marignano, Switzerland began to feel the influence of a man who was proclaiming that the country's real strength lay in the realm of the spirit. This man was a young Swiss priest, Ulrich Zwingli.

4

Conflict of Faith

I ZWINGLI AND THE REFORMATION

THE EMPIRE and the Papacy held the two great swords of power over men and their minds. As a result of the Swabian war, the Swiss Confederation had drifted farther away from the imperial throne than any other part of the Empire. At the same time, it had moved so close to the Papacy that the Pope had placed his life in the hands of Swiss Guards. Did he do so in the conviction that secularism would not penetrate to the heart of the Alpine valleys? Certainly in religious art, in liturgy and church drama, and in plain Christian charity, Swiss life reflected the simple faith of ordinary people. Nevertheless in Switzerland, as elsewhere, money was too often all-powerful. The rich and influential were drawing pensions from foreign powers for bartering the lives of poor mercenaries. Some of the clergy profiteered from simony and the Church was not concerned enough to restrain indulgence hawkers from offering the remission of sins for public sale. Rivalry between ecclesiastical orders led to miracle cults, with pilgrimages openly commercialised. The private lives of many priests were a disgrace, and their ignorance was so startling that it was said one had to search hard to find men of God who really knew their Bible.

The lack of erudition among the clergy, who were supposed to be the teachers of the people, became more obvious as intellectual curiosity increased in society as a whole. Since the invention of printing, books had become more easily accessible. It no longer took a life-time nor cost a fortune to reproduce a beautiful volume; in the time of Luther a printed Bible was no more expensive than a horse. At first, most of the works were printed in Latin, because the spirit of learning depended on the language of ancient Rome. Since the beginning of the Italian Renaissance in the 14th century, Rome and Greece had become the models for western scholarship in art, literature, political ideas and philosophy, with the emphasis on the potentialities of the individual human being.

The inspiration of the Renaissance was brought home to the Swiss as thousands of them became involved in the Milanese campaigns. Among them were artists, writers and skilled craftsmen, wood-carvers, glass-painters and architects. Another aspect of Renaissance ideas, humanism, found a home at Basle where the great humanist scholar Erasmus settled. It was at Basle, where Switzerland's oldest university had been founded in 1460, that works by Erasmus were printed by Johann Froben and exquisitely illustrated by Hans Holbein. And it was there in 1516 that Erasmus brought out his edition of the New Testament based on the Greek text. This edition was tremendously important as a manifesto of the new learning; and its clarification of the sources of the Christian faith greatly influenced two men who were embarking on the work of the Reformation. One was Martin Luther, who used the Erasmus New Testament as the foundation of his epoch-making translation into German, first published in 1522. The other was Ulrich Zwingli, who was setting out to preach the gospel in the new manner in Switzerland.

Zwingli is a classic example of three important influences on the Swiss character: the Alps, humanism and Christianity. He was born in a comfortably-off peasant family at Wildhaus, the highest village of Toggenburg in eastern Switzerland on 1 January 1484, less than two months after Luther's birth in Saxony. Zwingli made his acquaintance with humanism while at Vienna and Basle universities. As he reached maturity, Christianity became his all-embracing devotion. His first concern was not, like Luther's, personal salvation, but the care of his flock; and during his early priesthood, he saw what suffering could do to men when he served as a chaplain among the Swiss troops at Novara and Marignano. He began his tireless work as preacher, writer, teacher and social reformer in Glarus, where he was appointed parish priest at the age of 22. In social and political matters, he chafed at the evils of mercenary service and the acceptance of foreign pensions. He also deplored the way much of the good farming land was allowed to go to waste, and declared sternly: "Nobody any longer wants to earn his living by work." After Glarus, he spent two years as parish priest in the village of Einsiedeln, a centre of pilgrimage, where it was said he did not exactly set a shining example of discretion in his private life. From Einsiedeln, he moved on to undertake his great work in Zürich.

Ulrich Zwingli mounted the pulpit of the Grossmünster, the principal church of Zürich, on 1 January 1519, his 35th birthday. A large congregation heard him expound the St. Matthew gospel in a direct and individual style, without reference to the lessons prescribed by the Church. To him, the Bible alone was authority and guide in everything. The word of God, not ecclesiastical tradition, was his rule of faith. He spoke and wrote in favour of a simplified order of service, dispensing with images, pictures, ornament and legendary examples, a Church without the mass and monasticism. He attacked indulgences and opposed celibacy of the clergy; and within a few years he himself had married a young widow. In his sermons, he continued to deal with political issues like the traffic in Swiss troops, and as a result Zürich was the only part of the Confederation which did not sign an agreement in 1521 to supply mercenaries to France.

A devout and uncompromising Christian who deeply believed in divine justice, Zwingli nevertheless held that on earth it was for the temporal power to ensure that justice was done. In this he naturally found strong allies among the Zürich city councillors; and since the Church was doing little or nothing to put its house in order, the civic authority decided to step in. At the end of January 1523, the Great Council convened a public disputation at which Zwingli was given the opportunity to justify his policy of Church reform in the 67 Conclusions he drew up for the occasion. The official representative of the Bishop of Constance would not allow himself to be involved in the debate, however, and this induced the city council to give Zwingli official sanction to preach the gospel in his way and to initiate certain reforms. Later in 1523, a second disputation was held, directed by Zwingli's friend, the humanist Vadian from St. Gallen. The way was being cleared for the existing form of worship to be abolished in Zürich. At Easter 1525, communion was celebrated in the new manner for the first time.

Most of Zwingli's active supporters had their roots among the enlightened artisans, who believed that the clergy were no longer qualified to be in charge of welfare and education. The feeling was that the civic authorities could handle these matters just as well as the monasteries, which were now being dissolved. The city council made provision for the poor and for better popular education, with the Bible as the people's primer. The Zürich translation of 1530, the first complete Protestant Bible, was to supplement Luther's great version which was finished four years later. Great care was devoted to the training of priests, who were allowed to marry and were no longer regarded as the privileged mediators between God and man.

In his concern with social conditions, Zwingli deeply sympathised with the cause of the peasantry suffering under bondage which, they rightly argued, conflicted with the Biblical message that they were all God's children. Such an argument could not be as easily brushed aside by the authorities as the views of the Anabaptists, whose rebellion against the social order and rejection of infant baptism was answered with the death penalty. As a result of Zwingli's strong support for the peasants, Zürich introduced various reforms : bondage gradually disappeared on state-owned lands and more revenue was used for the benefit of the rural population. Zwingli's attitude contrasted sharply with that of Luther, who in 1525 urged ruthless action against peasant violence in Germany. To Luther, authority was ordained by God; and in a pamphlet which lost him a great deal of support he rashly declared there was nothing "more venomous, pernicious and Satanic" than a peasant insurgent. Here was an indication of the profound gulf between the two reformers. A few years later, at the Marburg conference of 1529, they clashed over the central problem of the interpretation of the Last Supper. Luther held that the body and blood of Christ co-existed with the consecrated elements, as fire is present in molten lead. But to Zwingli the communion in bread and wine was symbolical only and he rejected the concept of the Last Supper as a sacrament.

The leading towns of northern Switzerland followed the reformed faith : Zwingli's teaching was supported by the majority in Basle, Schaffhausen and St. Gallen, as well as in the Grisons, Glarus and Appenzell. But things were different in the heart of Switzerland. Schwyz, Uri, Unterwalden, Zug and Lucerne stuck to Catholicism, and there Zwingli ran into fierce opposition. The people of these cantons were not blind to the abuses of the Roman Church; and in Lucerne cantonal delegates met to seek a confederate solution to the schism. But the planned concordat between the two faiths did not materialise, partly because Zwingli was being opposed on more than religious grounds.

The resistance to him was in a sense politically motivated: the struggle was being conducted as a kind of new war against Zürich. In each generation people seemed to suspect the city of trying to dominate the rest of the Confederation. First there had been two burgomasters, Stüssi and later Waldmann, men of civic power who had finally been toppled. Now the danger came from the reformer Zwingli, who made no secret of his aims: a new alliance between Church and state which would enable him to be the prophet and guardian of Zürich. Already he was not only chief preacher, but adviser to the city in military and legal matters—"burgomaster, town clerk and city council all in one person" as Hans Salat, the Lucerne chronicler described him.

In the eyes of the forest cantons anyone who concentrated so much power in his hands was a danger to the Confederation as a whole, and this political conclusion reinforced their loyalty to Catholicism. Zwingli stayed away from a public disputation among the confederates at Baden in 1526; and the Catholics who were represented by Dr. Eck, a well-known opponent of Luther's, claimed to have won the day. But the year 1528 showed how meaningless this claim was. For now the powerful city of Berne joined the reformists, after a public debate which Zwingli made sure he did attend.

Berne's decision, far from counter-balancing the might of Zürich in the Protestant camp, simply buttressed it. The gulf between town and country, which Brother Klaus had bridged at Stans in 1481, had now opened up again over the religious issue. The cities of Zürich, Berne, Schaffhausen and Basle joined together in defence of the reformed faith. With them as allies were St. Gallen, Bienne, the free imperial city of Mühlhausen and Constance in south Germany. The five Catholic cantons replied by also seeking allies beyond the national borders, which now had less significance than the new barriers of religion. In April 1529 they accepted a "Christian Union" with Ferdinand of Austria. This alliance meant that in case of war the Protestants would have had to fight on two fronts against both the Catholic cantons and Habsburg, Switzerland's inveterate enemy.

To counter this Catholic move, the Lutheran Prince Philip of Hesse planned to bring the German and Swiss Protestants together in an alliance. Zwingli now saw the opportunity for settling accounts with the five Catholic cantons and he resolved to act quickly before they could receive military support from their allies. The five cantons had forbidden free preaching in the common lordships, whose jurisdiction also concerned the other confederates; and an evangelical preacher from Zürich, Jacob Kaiser, was burned as a heretic. At this, Zürich declared war. Many people in the city, however, counselled against this drastic step, and it was also opposed by the Bernese. Berne sent as an emissary Nicholas Manuel, who in his satirical plays had gone out of his way to mock Catholic pomp and luxury. But now he stepped before Zürich's rulers and beseeched them in God's name not to be so hot-headed. . . . "We cannot plant the faith in people's hearts," he declared, "with lance and halberd!"

Zwingli still pressed for action. But before Zürich's forces crossed the border with Zug in early summer 1529, his friend, the *Landamman* of Glarus, Johannes Aebli, managed to persuade him not to plunge the country into civil war. The troops were opposing each other at Kappel, but Aebli's mediation and Berne's refusal to support an offensive war against the Catholics had their effect : the encounter resolved itself into a legal squabble which was settled without any fighting at the first Peace of Kappel. The mediator tore up the agreement between the Habsburgs and the five Catholic cantons, while the cities were permitted to retain their new defensive alliance. In addition, each commune in the common lordships was given freedom to decide its own form of worship.

The Reformation continued its advance, and Zwingli still did not give up his aim of seeing that the gospel was preached freely in the Catholic cantons. The armed conflict was therefore only postponed. Zürich meanwhile hastened to consolidate its position on the Rhine and Lake Constance. In agreement with Glarus, it arbitrarily dissolved the monastery of St. Gallen; Zwingli's native area, Toggenburg, was temporarily given its *Landsgemeinde*; and so was Thurgau which under the influence of an evangelical *Landvogt* joined the reformists. Glarus and Zürich also gave all possible encouragement to the new teaching in the Linth valley, through which their border ran. This valley had been the bone of contention even in the first civil war. Once again the control of north-east Switzerland was at stake, and Zürich attempted to cut off the Catholic cantons from supplies by an economic blockade. It was the same tactic that had faced the mountain people before with the grim alternative of starvation or unyielding struggle.

Zwingli was set on seeing his plan through : he envisaged Zürich and Berne in harness as the driving force of the Confederation. This meant an assault on the equality and sovereignty of the individual cantons. A reform was involved which might have been justified in view of the great difference in the size of the Confederation's members; but Zwingli's ambition went much further. He visualised a grand Protestant federation embracing territories as far away as Friesland and Denmark. Indeed, though a sworn enemy of the mercenary system, he even contemplated recruiting mercenaries to carry out his scheme.

Zwingli had to pay the price for his ambition and the resort to arms. The end, when it came, was swift and astonishing. In October 1531, the five Catholic cantons declared war. Eight thousand men marched north from Zug towards Zürich. The city's forces were ill-prepared, outnumbered and incompetently led. At Kappel, on 11 October, they were overwhelmingly defeated. Zwingli, who had marched with them, was killed. His death, at the age of 47, was greeted by most people in the Catholic areas as a liberation from the man they called the *Vogt* of the entire Confederation, though some of them were prepared to admit that he was honest of purpose as well as tough and uncompromising.

It was Zwingli's tragedy that he was more eager than anyone else to unite the confederates and through this very eagerness drove them further apart. The second Peace of Kappel rescinded the reforms wherever they had been imposed under pressure. In addition, the Protestant cities were compelled to dissolve their alliance. The confederates anticipated the principle *cuius regio, eius religio* whereby each canton was to be allowed to decide and enforce its own form of religious observance. But in most of the common lordships where religion was mixed, Catholicism prevailed. The five Catholic cantons nevertheless showed sufficient political sense not to overrate their surprise victory at Kappel. Zürich, for its part, found in the young Heinrich Bullinger a trusted successor to Zwingli and one who proceeded with caution instead of the great reformer's impetuosity.

II   CALVIN IN GENEVA

Within a few years of Zürich's defeat and Zwingli's death, another
city emerged as the centre of a reformed faith which was destined to
acquire historic and widespread influence under the inspired guidance
of its founder. The city was French-speaking Geneva; the new leader
of reform, John Calvin.

At about the time that Zürich was in conflict with the Catholics,
Geneva was facing renewed pressure from the Duke of Savoy, who
claimed ancient imperial rights there. The city councillors had forged
protective links with the confederates in the shape of agreements with
Protestant Berne and Catholic Fribourg. When the threat from Savoy
grew, Bernese forces twice went to Geneva's aid, in 1530 and 1536,
and occupied Vaud, north of Lake Geneva. With the Bernese came
Protestant reformers, among them the Frenchman Guillaume Farel,
who worked to such purpose that the Catholic mass was suspended in
1536. At this point, John Calvin travelled through Geneva, intending
to stay only for a night. But Farel implored him, in God's name, to
remain among the worldly Genevese to help organise the reformed
Church. Calvin agreed to stay.

It was a change of plan with far-reaching consequences. For Calvin
was a clear, powerful thinker and a born organiser, trained in law,
theology and humanism. Because of his Protestant views, he had
become a refugee from his home in France; and in Basle earlier in
1536, he had published the first edition of his *Christianae religionis
institutio*, a masterly exposition of Protestant thought for a man of 26.
He and Farel set about drawing up the new Church's articles of
government, but they ran into opposition and in 1538 were both
forced to leave Geneva, Calvin going to Strasbourg where he married. But three years later his supporters in Geneva were strong
enough to get him invited back. He then proceeded with even
greater passion to carry out what he considered God's purpose and to
establish a kind of theocracy unparalleled for its rigorous discipline
and austerity. Sermons were preached every day. The churches were
crammed to overflowing. The consistory of pastors and elders kept an
inquisitorial eye on the citizens' daily lives. And when doctrinal disputes flared up, heretics were brought to trial.

Calvin was convinced that the city had a vital part to play in the world-wide dissemination of the reformed faith. The Academy of Geneva was founded to train the young. Two thousand of the city's 16,000 inhabitants were employed in 60 printing houses, publishing religious literature, primarily for distribution abroad. Calvin's ideas radiated to many countries, including Britain, France, the Netherlands, the Rhineland, and in due course North America. Sometimes the faith was carried by exiled foreigners who visited Geneva and worked in association with Calvin, men like John Knox, the leader of the reform movement in Scotland.

Though so intolerant in many ways, Calvin endeavoured to effect a compromise between the differing views of the Lutherans and Zwinglians, and was at least successful in achieving an agreement with the latter. He met Bullinger in 1549, and reached a doctrinal understanding with him which led to the Second Helvetic Confession and the drawing together of the reformed Church. So by the time of Calvin's death in 1564 at the age of 55, Geneva had created a close spiritual bond with Zürich just as it had forged political links with Berne in the face of the danger from Savoy. In 1602, Savoy made one last attack on Geneva, a night raid in which its soldiers were beaten off after scaling the city walls with ladders. The *escalade,* as it is known, was followed a year later by a peace agreement under which Savoy recognised the city's independence, though Geneva did not join the Confederation as a full member until 1815.

The Reformation had severely divided the Confederation. A majority of the cantons remained Catholic: Uri, Schwyz, Unterwalden, Zug, Lucerne, Fribourg and Solothurn. But the heavily populated cities were Protestant: Zürich, Basle, Berne and Schaffhausen, with the support of Geneva and a majority in the Grisons. A question mark hung over Glarus and Appenzell, as well as over the future canton of the Ticino, south of the Alps, and the common lordships. There were other factors, however. Although the Reformation had caused divisions within the German-speaking cantons, the emergence of Calvin's Geneva meant that a bridge had been built to the French-speaking communities. Moreover, the fact that two religions balanced each other was a deterrent against the whole Confederation becoming involved in the religious wars which were to cause so much bloodshed and suffering in Europe. If religious division was not to lead to political dismemberment, it was a matter of common interest

to all the Swiss to keep out of the struggles beyond their borders. So
Switzerland's neutrality was to become a necessity, consolidated in the
years of European conflict.

III   COUNTER-REFORMATION

Switzerland fortunately escaped becoming a battlefield in the European religious wars. But with refugees streaming into the country, the
Swiss were brought face to face with the suffering of their European
neighbours. They were, moreover, inevitably caught up in the counter-
reformation, in which the Catholic Church aimed at restoring its
image, authority and power and preventing the further spread of
Protestantism.

A great gathering for the purification of the Catholic Church, the
Council of Trent (1545–1563) was held in the Tyrol, not far from
Switzerland's borders. The reforms it accepted were as important to
the Swiss as to other countries where abuses had undermined the
prestige of the Church. The Swiss also felt the impact of the new
religious orders which promoted the purposes of the counter-reformation—above all, the highly-disciplined and erudite Jesuits and the
more widely popular Capuchins. The Jesuits trained their priests for
work in education, research and diplomacy, establishing centres in
Lucerne and Fribourg, where a great Catholic reformer, the Dutch-
man Peter Canisius, spent the last years of his life. The main concern
of the Capuchins was to carry the new spirit to the people of the
villages and to care for their needs; and the Capuchin monks came
to establish monasteries in Schwyz, Lucerne, Sion and elsewhere.

But perhaps the greatest name in the counter-reformation in
Switzerland is Carlo Borromeo, the young Cardinal Archbishop of
Milan, who was a driving force in the revival of Catholicism among
the Swiss with whom he was in direct contact through his diocesan
work. Borromeo was the nephew of Pius IV, who symbolised a new
style of Papacy and finally brought the Council of Trent to a successful conclusion. The work of revival in Switzerland was also carried
forward by the first papal nuncio there, Giovanni Francesco
Bonhomini, and by the foundation of the Helvetian college in Milan,
where future priests could be trained.

Among the thousands of persecuted Protestants from other lands who sought refuge in Switzerland were some of those who left England during the reign of Mary Tudor, in the face of her attempt to restore the realm to Catholicism. But the religious intolerance which affected the Swiss most directly was that in neighbouring France, which culminated in the Massacre of St. Bartholomew on 24 August 1572. This orgy of killing cost the lives of several thousand Protestants, the Huguenots—whose name is believed to be a distortion of the word *Eidgenossen*, the "sworn compatriots" of Switzerland. Many of those who escaped the slaughter knew where their spiritual home lay: 2,300 families fled to Geneva, the city of refuge. They were given immediate assistance; and the city even offered permanent shelter within its walls to more than two-thirds of their number, which was about half the size of its own population. Among the refugees there were many skilled craftsmen, who helped to found the local clock-making industry. Geneva was not the only Protestant city to benefit from the contribution of the new immigrants to commercial life. In Basle, the Huguenots established lace-making, and religious refugees from the south brought their skills in silk dyeing and the manufacture of velvet. The textile industry of Zürich owed its growing prosperity chiefly to Protestant exiles from Locarno who, in 1555, had been faced by the Catholic majority with the choice of abandoning either their faith or their homes.

While the arrival of the Protestant refugees strengthened the Swiss in one way, the Catholic counter-reformation enriched them in another by re-awakening traditional piety. Once again the churches were full, and many new ones were built. The Valais, the Grisons and the Ticino abound in examples of this enthusiastic revival of church building, and architects and craftsmen from these cantons were among the leading pioneers of Italian and Bavarian Baroque. The imposing abbeys of St. Gallen and Einsiedeln are lasting testimonies to this inspiration and skill. Yet although it brought enrichment and beauty, Catholic revival in Switzerland was not accomplished without violent conflict, even if it was not on the scale of the religious wars in France and Germany.

The drive to secure the aims of the counter-reformation met with particular opposition in the canton of Glarus, where the reformed faith had won many adherents since Ulrich Zwingli began his priesthood there. The chief Catholic campaigner was Aegidius Tschudi, who is known for his confederate history, *Chronicon Helveticum,* of the years up to 1470. By learned argument, intrigue and force he sought to bring the evangelical congregations back to the faith of Rome. This pressure was kept up for four years, and "Tschudi's War"—as it is popularly called—nearly led to another civil war. But ultimately in 1564 a measure of security was restored to the Protestant minority, after Zürich and Berne had intervened on their behalf.

Another dispute arose in Appenzell, which was one of several areas whose constitutional and religious position had not been adequately settled in the Peace of Kappel of 1531. Here the situation was closely affected by the work of Cardinal Borromeo whose activities greatly encouraged the Catholic cantons' religious policy. In 1586 an alliance known as the Borromean League was formed by Uri, Schwyz, Unterwalden, Lucerne, Zug, Fribourg and Solothurn. Appenzell's position presented a problem : was it to join the League? The controversy was not solved until 11 years later when the canton was divided into two separate areas on denominational grounds—the Inner (Catholic) and Outer (Protestant) Rhodes.

Meanwhile, the Borromean League had entered into an agreement with Philip II of Spain, who was promised a supply of soldiers and free passage for his forces across League territories. Philip, son of the Habsburg Emperor Charles V and ruler of widespread lands including Milan, was engaged in furthering the Catholic cause and strengthening his hand in his campaign against France. When he died in 1598, his anti-French mission was still unaccomplished, and later Habsburgs were left to renew the struggle in the disastrous war of the next century.

IV   WAR AND SOVEREIGNTY

The Thirty Years War, which devastated Germany between 1618 and 1648, arose out of a religious revolt in Bohemia, turned into a power contest between France and the Habsburgs, and ended with a French victory. The war seemed bound to involve the Swiss Confederation, and many of its mercenaries did go off to fight on either side. But the official policy—and the only one to prevent the religiously-divided Confederation being dragged into the turmoil and broken up—was to stay neutral. Yet to have even a chance of defending its neutrality

Ulrich Zwingli (1484–1531), leader of the Reformation in German-speaking Switzerland, killed in battle against the Catholics.

John Calvin (1509–1564), the great
reformer who made Geneva a citadel of the
Protestant faith.

Jean Jacques Rousseau (1712–1778), born in Geneva where his father was a watchmaker. His epoch-making book *The Social Contract* was published in 1760.

Part of the pageant of Swiss history: the
Council of the Two Hundred in Berne file
away from a meeting in the Town Hall.

against violation by the belligerent countries, Switzerland would have needed a strong national army. It was not until 1647 that, after long argument, a central force of 12,000 men was established by the Defensionale of Wyl—an agreement, named after the place where it was drawn up, which marked the beginning of the armed neutrality of Switzerland.

Before this stage was reached, the war had been dragging on for 29 years and Swiss neutrality had often been violated by the belligerents. Swedish troops, for example, entered the country during the siege of Constance, and another area where there was continual trouble from foreign intervention was the Grisons. The French and Venice on the one hand, and Austria and Spain on the other, had quarrelled for decades over the strategic passes there; and the acute problem this caused was made even more difficult when the Catholic population of Valtellina rebelled against the Protestant majority. In the end Jörg Jenatsch—a militant Protestant pastor turned Catholic for political reasons—helped to rid the canton of the foreigners. But Jenatsch's colourful career ended with the violence of the age: he was murdered in 1639.

After thirty years of war, an exhausted Europe laid down its arms in 1648. The Peace of Westphalia was a significant stage in the development of the nation—states of Europe, and the decline of imperial and religious power as it had been known. It was fitting that Swiss neutrality should be given its reward in the settlement. The peace conference, in which the Basle burgomaster Rudolf Wettstein played an influential role as one of the Protestant mediators, accepted a clause giving legal recognition to Switzerland's sovereignty and complete independence from the Empire. This outcome was not only heartening to the Swiss, who had enjoyed independence in practice since the Swabian war; it also met the wishes of France to see Switzerland separated from the Empire once and for all.

In Switzerland, religious strife had started earlier than in other parts of Europe; and although it had subsided during the Thirty Years War, it was to drag on longer than elsewhere. The religious division continued to stand in the way of a more equitable political and economic structure of the loosely-linked Confederation. Ever since the defeat at Kappel in 1531 the Protestant cantons had been in a politically inferior position. Although they embraced a larger section of the population and were economically much stronger, they were fewer in number than the Catholic cantons and could thus be out-voted in the Diet whenever it debated the administration of the common lordships and any direct threats to the Confederation as a whole. The Protestants found this situation unbearable, but were unsuccessful in efforts to get it remedied.

Twice, in 1656 and 1712, religious tension caused relatively minor issues to flare up into conflicts. These were the Villmergen Wars, named after the location of the main battles. As a result of the first campaign, the Catholics retained their predominant position in the Diet. But in the second, the Protestants were victorious. This second dispute is sometimes called the Toggenburg War because one of its causes was a Catholic plan to build a road from Schwyz through the Protestant Toggenburg valley to the Austrian frontier, thus cutting off Zürich from the Protestants of Glarus. The local people refused to carry out the scheme and were supported in their resistance by Zürich and Berne. The Peace of Aarau in 1712 ensured the Protestants equal religious rights in the common lordships and secured them parity of numbers on tribunals which settled disputes.

The Aarau arrangement left not only the Swiss Catholics dissatisfied. France, too, was affected. The French had a powerful say in Swiss affairs—offering military employment to mercenaries, supplying vital raw materials and providing important markets for Swiss goods. In 1715 they drew up a secret agreement with the Catholic cantons and their allies promising them French support in any dispute within the Confederation. The pact, which was known as the *Trücklibund*, was however not put into effect and the Protestants retained the advantages secured in the Peace of Aarau. One of the significant results of the Peace was to increase the territorial strength of both Zürich and Berne. The power of the cities, and particularly Berne, was an important factor in the social unrest of the 17th and 18th centuries and the decline of the old Confederation.

5

The Years of Decline

I PEASANT RISING

THE ORIGINAL Confederation had been founded by the Alpine peasants of the forest cantons, who had successfully defended their liberties against outsiders. In contrast, the peasantry of the plateau had suffered a harsher political fate, falling mostly under the expanding power of Berne. At one time, the villages in the area had enjoyed a good deal of self-government; and even during the Reformation period they were consulted on matters of major importance and had some say in the policy of the city. But the patrician rulers of Berne later became increasingly autocratic, and this trend was followed elsewhere. The countrymen under city control found themselves reduced to the status of subject peoples, ruled by right of conquest. Their liberties were whittled away, consultation went by the board, and they felt oppressed by harsh taxation. The aim of the cities was to centralise their power. The village people, on the other hand, wanted to save something of the communal and federal system and a minimum of living democracy. The peasant rising in 1653 was an attempt to assert the rights of the villages against city power: it was to be the last determined attempt to do so during the life of the old Confederation.

The peasants were finally driven to rebellion by economic pressures after the end of the Thirty Years War. They had done very well out of the war in its early years. Refugees had streamed into Switzerland to settle there in safety; the increased demand for food meant that farmers secured high prices; and foreign settlers with money were prepared to invest any amount of it in land and houses. The value of farm property soared and peasant prosperity was enhanced. But when peace came, this trend was reversed. Many of the war-time immigrants began to leave Switzerland, and food prices and property values dropped as they put their estates on the market. Swiss buyers showed little interest in the land made available, since they were hardly able to sell their own produce on a now listless market. The peasants were quick to blame their rulers for the inevitable worsening of their economic conditions. The city of Berne added to the discontent by a far-reaching and ill-conceived move : towards the end of 1652 it devalued the currency by 50 per cent and allowed a mere three days for the payment of debts to the treasury in the old money. This was utterly inadequate and put people like mountain farmers of the Oberland at a great disadvantage. Despite such obvious injustices, the Diet extended the Bernese regulations to the whole of Switzerland.

These decisions were the signal for rebellion. It broke out first in the valley of Entlebuch adjoining Unterwalden, one of the forest cantons which had long shown the meaning of a free peasantry. The village people of Entlebuch assembled in their *Landsgemeinden* not to clamour for a share in government, let alone for complete self-rule, but to make the simple demand to the city rulers for a return to the days when villagers' views were properly considered before legislation. The rebels' call was taken up elsewhere. In due course, meetings were held at Sumiswald and Huttwil, where 3,000 people gathered, both Catholic and Protestant, from the regions of Berne, Lucerne and Basle. Soon a Peasants' Union was confronting a Union of the Lords. And the rebellion had meanwhile found its leader : Nicholas Leuenberger, a man of immense popularity among the peasants who idolised him wherever he appeared in his striking red cloak.

Some 16,000 peasants marched behind Leuenberger to fight for greater autonomy. They appeared before the gates of Berne and laid siege to it for a week, finally forcing the city's rulers to agree to their demands. The other cities were naturally alarmed at these developments; and the free peasants of the forest cantons also took fright. They, too, had acquired subject territories, in which they feared the danger of a rising, and they therefore decided to throw in their lot with the cities. In three engagements the peasant insurgents, sometimes armed only with scythes, were crushed by the forces of the Lords' Union. Exploiting the situation, Berne went back on the undertakings it had given to the peasants. Their leaders were tortured and executed. The Diet, conscience-stricken, decided on certain reforms, but these offered little guarantee of a genuine improvement in the lot of the peasants in subject territories. Even though their condition was not so bad as in some other countries, the village remained under the will of the city for another 150 years.

II THE AGE OF ABSOLUTISM

The peasant rising threw into focus the political and social divisions in Switzerland, and the effect on it of the spirit of absolutism in Europe. By the 17th and 18th centuries, both the structure of the Confederation and social relationships within it had become extremely complicated. The old Confederation was not a state in the modern sense, but a loose association of cantons and territories, greatly varying in power and status. It was led by the 13 cantons, controlling subject territories and themselves ordered into a certain hierarchy. Zürich, Berne and Lucerne, followed by the three forest cantons, had precedence over the other members. Then there were the allies (*Zugewandte Orte*), like the Grisons and St. Gallen, held together by an elaborate web of treaties and traditions. Lower down the line were those which ranked in a sense as protectorates, such as the village republic of Gersau on Lake Lucerne and the principality of Neuchâtel. And then there were the common lordships, each of which was jointly governed by the group of cantons which had conquered it. The position of the common lordships was vital to the defence of the Confederation as a whole because they were potential bridgeheads for any attack on it and their administration depended on unity of purpose among the cantons which governed them.

No effective central control existed in the Confederation. There was no federal army, no federal treasury, and strictly speaking no federal law. The Diet was not a parliament in the modern sense, but rather a congress of representatives from the cantons who voted in accordance with instructions from home. When new and unexpected problems cropped up, they had to seek a fresh mandate. The Diet was not able to create new law by majority decision, and even unanimous decisions acquired legal validity only after approval and ratification by the cantons.

The country was governed as variously as can be imagined. There were autocratic rulers, hereditary oligarchies and popular assemblies,

depending on the territory. Even where traditional democratic practices continued, as in the forest cantons with their *Landsgemeinden*,
only prominent families were habitually chosen for important posts.
The anti-democratic trend was only too evident in the cities. In
Berne, Lucerne, Solothurn and Fribourg, political power was in the
hands of a patriciate, consisting of a few wealthy, privileged families.
Zürich, Basle, Schaffhausen and St. Gallen, on the other hand, were
ruled by craft guilds, but entry to the ranks of the guild-masters was
limited.

The whole Confederation was inevitably affected by the absolutist
spirit of the age. With the Swiss doing mercenary service at the courts
of foreign rulers, it was perhaps not surprising that many of those in
authority at home should behave like petty autocrats towards their
own subjects. This was a betrayal of the original ideals of self-
government in the Confederation, which was now rent not only by
religious divisions but by an ever-deepening social gulf. It was only a
question of time before this split between rulers and subjects would
paralyse the Confederation, if not break it up altogether.

A spirit of selfishness had resulted in the cantons setting their faces
against accepting new members of the Confederation. They were too
keen to keep the spoils of foreign mercenary service to themselves.
They were also loath to share with any newcomers the material benefits which they derived from the joint administration of the common
lordships. Within the cantons, the aristocratic families, the guilds, and
the citizenry closed their doors to new contenders for power. Even
the *Landsgemeinden* were known to prevent under-privileged immigrants from obtaining citizenship for decades, either by demanding
extortionate payments or by a formal ban. In relations with the
subject territories, there was a failure to recognise that if something
had been done to improve the status of their peoples, the internal
strength of the whole country would have been greatly enhanced.

In the atmosphere of the Confederation at this time, particular
attention centres on Berne, the city against which the peasant rising
had been aimed and which was to know further abortive rebellion
against its paternalistic rule. Berne came to be governed by no more
than a few dozen families, who divided among themselves the 200
chairs of the city's Great Council and the 50 rural governorships.
These offices were decided by lot, and to each winner they brought in

six annual payments of between 13,000 and 18,000 francs. It was from this lottery and the money received from mercenaries on foreign military service that the ruling oligarchy built themselves magnificent Baroque and Rococo residences, while at the same time equipping the city with a magnificent granary, the Kander canal and a network of avenues. The language and fashion was French and Versailles set the tone, but Protestant sobriety and a sense of responsibility were markedly different from the atmosphere at the court of the Bourbons. This contrast prompted Goethe later in the 18th century to laud not only the cleanliness and beauty of Berne but what he called the "equality among the citizens." Those who did not belong to the small ruling clique would have had something different to say about that.

One of those who rebelled against this narrow preserve of privilege, among families who were often inter-related, was a cultured Bernese named Samuel Henzi. He organised a conspiracy to democratise the city regime and to improve the legal and economic position of the rural people. But his plans came to a tragic end. The plot was betrayed, and Henzi and the other ringleaders were executed in 1749. Another idealist, Major Davel, had earlier paid with his life for a similarly abortive attempt to obtain self-government for his native French-speaking territory of Vaud.

The instability of the Confederation, dramatised by incidents such as these, would not have been a cause for despair if the ancient loyalty of its members had stood the test of time. The heroic period of Swiss history had proved that the undefined bond between them was far more important than the written letter of a constitution. In the past, the confederates had been united because they had a common enemy. But for a long time now they had shared the questionable blessing of a common friend—the king of France. The French monarch was out to prevent their squabbles blowing up into civil war, not just because he fancied himself as the most Christian of kings but because he did not want them to exhaust themselves in domestic conflict. What mattered to him was that Swiss mercenaries should at all times be available to France.

Although the Confederation was now weak and powerless internally, Swiss soldiers were still held in high esteem abroad for their fighting skill. France sought to enlist her former enemies in her own forces, and the French court was lavish with gifts. Louis XIV set particular store by a mercenary service agreement signed in 1663 at Solothurn, the residence of the French Ambassador, by all the cantons and allies, and solemnly ratified two months later at Notre Dame in Paris. Although the pact envisaged that Louis XIV could use 6,000 to 16,000 mercenaries for defensive purposes only, he was planning various offensive campaigns; and within less than a decade the French War Minister, Louvois, had set up the first permanent Swiss regiment within the French army, thus ensuring France a free hand in the use of the mercenaries.

To capable and ambitious Swiss soldiers, enlistment in such permanent regiments opened a military career irrespective of the rank and influence of their families at home. The freedom to join foreign armies sometimes led to tragic situations. At the battle of Malplaquet in 1709 during the Spanish War of Succession, Swiss mercenaries in French service were engaged in ferocious fighting with their compatriots recruited by the Dutch. Three centuries of war are calculated to have involved some two million Swiss soldiers—an unprecedented drain of national strength in mercenary service. Other solutions to the problem of surplus manpower and unemployment were not found until merchants followed in the steps of the mercenaries. New markets abroad were gradually opened up to such Swiss trades as the linen manufacture of St. Gallen. Only then could work be provided for the young peasants outside the farm and the battlefield. Meanwhile, mercenary service went on, and the situation had changed paradoxically from the past. The founders of the Confederation, as members of a people's army, had taken up arms against the professional military caste of the Middle Ages. Their descendants had now become professional soldiers themselves, shedding their blood in defence of absolute government.

The Confederation was in a sense brought to the brink of serfdom. But there was hope of freedom in new political ideas circulating in Europe. The most stirring of these ideas came from the pen of Jean Jacques Rousseau of Geneva.

6

A New Beginning

I ROUSSEAU AND PESTALOZZI

THE GREAT French statesman Talleyrand is credited with the remark that there were five continents: Europe, Asia, America, Africa—and Geneva. He must have been thinking of the profound international influence both of Calvinism and of the political gospel of Jean Jacques Rousseau, who was born in Geneva in 1712.

Rousseau made his outstanding contribution to political philosophy between 1750 and 1762, the year which saw the publication of *The Social Contract*. This work contains virtually Rousseau's entire political theory and an exposition of the principles which he regards as the essential foundation of every legitimate society. He says the sole basis of such a society is the will of its members; it exists by the consent of the people and is based on a contract among them. The people are sovereign; the government is not their master but their servant and can always be deposed. What Rousseau calls the General Will is the source of all laws in the state and is directed solely to the common good: the first principle and fundamental rule of government is the supremacy of this General Will. Rousseau expresses a belief in the essential goodness of human nature and gives voice to the aspirations for political and economic equality in a society in which human freedom flourishes.

These ideas of Rousseau's became, as it were, the Bible of the French Revolution. They produced a ringing echo among the enlightened bourgeoisie and revolutionaries of France, undermined the moral position of absolutist princes, and were bound to heighten discontent in Switzerland at the privileged status of its own aristocracy. The Berne government had Rousseau's books burnt and forced him to leave St. Peter's Island on Lake Bienne. But no government was able to suppress his ideas.

Rousseau, the son of a watchmaker in Geneva, owed a considerable debt to his native city-state, and this he acknowledged in the long dedication to his *Discourse on the Origin of Inequality*. He paid Geneva this tribute: "How could I reflect on the equality which nature has ordained between men, and the inequality which they have introduced, without reflecting on the profound wisdom by which both are in this state happily combined and made to coincide, in the manner that is most in conformity with natural law, and most favourable to society, to the maintenance of public order and to the happiness of individuals?" The citizens' assembly of Geneva, which was akin in spirit to the old Alpine *Landsgemeinden*, influenced Rousseau in his thinking; and by drawing attention to the assembly's work he showed the world what Switzerland had at its best achieved politically. Similarly, as a poet he opened his contemporaries' eyes to the beauty of the Swiss mountains.

At the dawn of a new era, in life and letters as well as in political affairs, the romantic appeal of Switzerland's landscape and the best qualities of its social life began to make themselves felt. Among the great foreign writers attracted by it were Edmund Gibbon, who lived at Lausanne for many years while writing *The Decline and Fall of the Roman Empire*, and Voltaire who made his home by Lake Geneva and in the Swiss-French borderland. The quest for a society based on reason and justice which engaged Voltaire's energies put him in the forefront of those writers to whose inspiration the entire Enlightenment owed such a great debt. He contributed to Diderot's famous *Encyclopédie*, which aimed at promoting a cultural revolution in France; he lived for a while at the court of Frederick the Great of Prussia, exposing that enlightened despot to the originality of his mind; and in his work he championed tolerance, justice and reason.

The French philosophers of the Enlightenment like Voltaire and Montesquieu, who were determined to defeat dogma, superstition and ignorance by the superior powers of critical reason, were particularly impressed by what they had seen on visits to England. The level-headed British relied above all on experience and common-sense. To them absolutism seemed nonsense; the power of their king was limited; the dignity of the individual was respected; and there was far greater freedom of thought than on the Continent. Voltaire, in a tribute to the great English philosopher John Locke, said of him that he displayed the workings of human reason as an anatomist unfolds the mechanism of the body. Locke, writing at the end of the 17th century at about the time of the revolution against James II, had proclaimed man's natural right to liberty, life and property. Little more than half a century later, Montesquieu published his great work on the principles of government, *De l'Esprit des Lois*. He held that the spirit of the laws is determined by natural and social conditions; and he expressed his admiration for the constitutional government and monarchy in England where he saw a clear separation of legislative, executive and judicial powers. Montesquieu made an immense impression, and in Switzerland was almost as influential as Rousseau.

These ideas for reforming human society recognised no boundaries. They linked thinking men of diverse backgrounds in absolutist France, in constitutional England, and in Switzerland, where the ancient *Landsgemeinden* were rooted in democracy. At this time, there were forces at work among the Swiss seeking to purify the country and bring it back to its original ideals. A passionately patriotic group of men, most of them dedicated to the Enlightenment and the triumph of reason, got together to strive for the country's regeneration and unity. In 1761, they met at Schinznach Spa on the river Aare and founded the Helvetic Society, with a programme for the rejuvenation of the old Confederation. The author of the plan, the Lucerne city-councillor Franz Urs Balthasar, was enthusiastically acclaimed in Zürich, Basle, Berne and elsewhere. Balthasar believed that salvation could first come from a responsibly educated, patriotic aristocracy. He also advocated closer links among the confederates and a federal army; and soon demands were heard for a unitary state whose citizens would enjoy equal rights and obligations.

By contrast to the Economic Society of Berne, which set in train the abolition of some outdated agricultural practices, most of the Helvetic Society's ideas remained mere dreams and abstract projects. Yet the Society was the meeting ground of enlightened men, indeed the sole national forum of intellectual leaders whose role in Swiss history was properly appreciated only in later times. Its members included the "peasant-philosopher" Jakob Guyer, known as Kleinjogg; the Christian poet and thinker, Johann Kaspar Lavater, who recited some of his poems on liberty and national unity to the gatherings; and the historian Johannes von Müller, who read out the early chapters of his celebrated *History of the Swiss Confederation* in which he sought to re-awaken the country's faith in its original ideals. Patriots and idealists though they were, the men of the Helvetic Society were not blind to the practical shortcomings of Switzerland; and Müller himself once called the "much-vaunted freedom of the Swiss a phantom—a thing of naught."

The country's most immediate need was its inward regeneration, and the member of the Helvetic Society who perhaps saw this most clearly was the great educationist and patriot Johann Heinrich Pestalozzi (1746–1827). In this respect, Pestalozzi was a realist even though many of his schemes did not work out in practice. He deeply believed that a morally healthy society can evolve only from a healthy family, where the process of all education has to begin and which is the "sanctuary" for the regeneration of the community and the state. In his popular book *Lienhard und Gertrud,* Pestalozzi opened his countrymen's eyes to this concept. His approach differed greatly from the educational ideas of Rousseau, whose influential work *Emile* was published when Pestalozzi was a boy of 15. In the story, Rousseau has his Emile brought up outside the family and seems almost to overlook its importance as a nucleus of the community. For Pestalozzi— the father of the Swiss primary school—the home always came before the classroom, although he did not underrate formal instruction. On the relation between education and a democratic community he wrote: "Without political education the sovereign people is like a child playing with fire and constantly endangering the home."

Switzerland at the time of the Helvetic Society certainly had its able scholars, just as in the 16th century it had produced men like the great physician Paracelsus and the naturalist Konrad Gesner. But the Swiss did not give scholars their due, as was shown in the university city of Basle, where complaints were heard that a man of learning counted barely as much as an unskilled labourer. Yet for decades it had been Basle scholars, especially members of the amazing Bernoulli family of mathematicians, who had submitted prize-winning contributions to the Academy of Paris; and in St. Petersburg, they referred to a "Basle Legion" of intellectuals, headed by the distinguished mathematician Leonard Euler. Another great Swiss, the Bernese Albrecht von Haller, who was among the first to reveal to his generation the magnificence of the Alpine world in his poem *The Alps,* also learned how little his countrymen appreciated intellectual achievement. Acclaimed abroad for his contribution to natural sciences, especially anatomy, Haller found it difficult to attain even relatively minor posts in his homeland.

Zürich, too, was ungenerous. It made no more than a miserable offer of money, corn and wine to the young Johann Jakob Scheuchzer, who had been recommended by the German philosopher and mathematician Leibniz. Peter the Great had offered Scheuchzer the post of personal physician; but despite this tempting opportunity he stayed in Zürich and helped with the intellectual groundwork which encouraged the growth of Pestalozzi's ideas and the flowering of the pastoral poetry of Salomon Gessner. Such groundwork was invaluable, but the more far-sighted Swiss knew that much still had to be accomplished before the thinkers and the poets could bring about a change in the social landscape. An Appenzell doctor, Laurenz Zellweger, who had been involved in a popular uprising in his canton earlier in the century, was not the only one in despair about the decline of the country. Zellweger expressed what many were thinking when he wrote a letter to Johann Jakob Bodmer, a Zürich scholar with radical political ideas, and declared : "We are heading straight towards ruin."

II   THE TORCH OF REVOLUTION

The educated Swiss, whether or not they shared the forebodings of ruin, could hardly fail to be concerned by what was going on in France, with whom relations had been so close for centuries. It was not for nothing that the French kept their ambassador at Solothurn : the style in which he held court constantly reminded the Swiss that there was money to be earned when his king needed mercenaries. The poor knew that he could sometimes be relied upon to throw coins from his window to the crowd in the street. But more important was the gold that found its way into the pockets of his distinguished visitors in return for the promise to supply mercenary troops. In 1777, the tiny Swiss states and the kingdom of the Bourbons solemnly reaffirmed their mercenary service agreement at the St. Ursus church in Solothurn—and it was an arrangement that still served both parties well. To the adventurous young Swiss, for whom their homeland found it difficult to provide employment, soldiering was a vital source of income; and France was the more dependent on them the less her nobles at the Court of Versailles were inclined to exchange their dress swords for the weapons of battle.

No Swiss serving with the French could miss the contrast in the relations between state and people in France and in his homeland. The Confederation, whatever its shortcomings, presented a picture of diversity in its institutions and in its social, intellectual and religious life, while the French rulers sought to impose a pattern of uniformity on everything. The Swiss jealously guarded against any single canton or individual gaining too great an ascendancy over the others. Paris, in its splendour, contemptuously treated the rest of France as a mere province; and at Versailles absolutism was enthroned, with a king who behaved as if he were a demi-god.

There were, of course, deep class divisions in Switzerland as well. The differences, however, were less marked than in a country of 25 million people, where two-thirds of the land belonged to one-fortieth of the population—the nobility and the Church. Yet the taxes paid by these two privileged estates in France bore no relation to their wealth; and few people any longer accepted the excuse that the aristocracy were making their national contribution in battle and the clergy in prayer. In these conditions of inequality it was particularly obnoxious that large amounts of revenue disappeared into the pockets of tax gatherers, and that up to 50 million francs a year were squandered by frivolous women of the court. The French peasants had to give up as much as four-fifths of their income in taxes or dues; yet here was the king with a whole regiment of bodyguards and 4,000 servants at his beck and call! Money earned by hard sweat was being frittered away on pomp and luxury, while the peasants' own families were starving. The people had been described by Louis XIV—*le roi soleil*—as the "rabble"; and one French minister called them "a sponge to be squeezed dry."

Such was the arrogance that brought the old regime into final conflict with those who took their stand by the ideals of Rousseau and his demand that all power must lie with the people. The writings of the champions of liberty and equality had profoundly influenced those of the middle class who were yearning for an age in which these ideas would be given reality. There was, after all, living proof that the principles of freedom could be expressed as the will of an entire nation : for this was exactly what the Americans had done in 1776 by enshrining the Rights of Man in their Declaration of Independence. Rousseau's dictum of the sovereignty of the people had become political fact. But was that possible only in the New World?

Some changes of attitude had been accomplished in France without bloodshed; and if the court showed enough foresight there was still a chance of diverting the flood of discontent into the channels of orderly reform. In 1789, after a series of financial crises, Louis XVI felt it necessary to summon the States-General for the first time for 175 years. The 1,200 deputies—nobles, clergy and representatives of the third estate—assembled at Versailles in May to discuss the country's critical finances. What the king wanted was money to bridge the yawning deficit. But would he offer reforms in return? The third estate was in no mood merely to pay up. It waited to hear word of the king's intentions, and waited in vain for encouragement. In June, the deputies of the third estate declared themselves to constitute the National Assembly, and swore not to separate until they had given France a constitution.

In July, the king dismissed his finance minister, the celebrated Genevese banker Jacques Necker, who had been advising concessions. After this, the fear of counter-revolution grew among the people of Paris, and the demand on the streets was for drastic action. On 14 July the ancient prison fortress of the Bastille was stormed. In October, the mob forced the king to forsake Versailles for Paris, where he was lodged in the Tuileries, the old royal palace. The revolution was taking its turbulent course. The privileges of the nobility and the clergy were abolished; and by 1792, after an abortive attempt by the king to escape, his end was not far off. On 10 August the mob stormed the Tuileries and tried to drag Louis XVI and his family into the streets. Seven-hundred and fifty Swiss Guards honoured their pledge of loyalty and defended the palace until ordered by the king to cease fire. In the massacre that followed most of them were hacked to pieces. A few months later, in January 1793, the king lay beneath the guillotine. His death, and the Terror to follow, horrified Europe.

To the people of Paris, the fall of the Bastille had symbolised the dawn of liberty and equality proclaimed in the first revolutionary constitution, which declared that sovereignty resides in the people. In a country like Switzerland, too, the watchwords "liberty, fraternity and equality" aroused the hope of better times among all those who were in any way under-privileged—and that meant seven-eighths of the Swiss population. The ruling classes, in contrast, sensed a clear danger of a conflagration on their own soil in which established order would be destroyed. And those Swiss Guards who escaped the massacre at the Tuileries must have wondered about a liberty that could so easily turn into unrestrained mob rule. Did a people such as the Swiss do better to prepare their country gradually for a greater degree of freedom, and was there still time to do so? The issue the Swiss now had to face was how far they and their institutions would be caught up in their great neighbour's revolution and whether their unity and tradition of neutrality could stand the test in the European war which had broken out against France.

III THE FRENCH INVASION

The Paris revolutionaries did not intend their ideas to stop at the French frontier. The rights of man belonged to all humanity, and the mission of spreading the word was undertaken with religious fervour. The message was: "We are free; follow our example." It appeared on leaflets which 3,000 pigeons were to carry abroad, while on foreign soil below revolutionary agents and supporters were burrowing away.

Idealism was one thing; but with it often went a lust for power. As events gathered speed, it turned out to be a brief journey from the freedom tree—erected to symbolise the growth of liberty—to the guillotine. And many idealistic supporters of the early revolution were hounded along that path during the Terror. Before their turn came, the crowned heads had rolled; the Church, too, was toppled from its position of power. Religion was denied in the name of reason; the Christian calendar was replaced by one dating from the inception of the new republic.

Among the established rulers of Church and state in Europe, the new calendar and the new world concept aroused alarm and fear and a growing determination to resist the revolutionary gospel. The Habsburg dynasty, which had made its peace with the Bourbons, once again became the enemy of France. Prussia, too, and then Britain

joined in the European struggle against the French which was to last
for nearly 25 years. It was in a sense a struggle between two worlds
and two generations. The average age of the coalition generals opposing France was over 70. The French generals who called the whole
nation to arms were under 40, and the youngest of them was the most
brilliant: Napoleon Bonaparte. At the start of the revolution, he was
just 20; only seven years later he led an army through north Italy
to the southern borders of Switzerland.

Revolutionary ideas had gained much sympathy among educated
people in Switzerland, but revolutionary excesses caused second
thoughts. The Swiss in general were resentful when republican France
dishonoured old agreements by discharging the mercenaries and sending them home; and the whole country continued to mourn the
victims of the furious mob which had attacked the Tuileries. All who
believed in order—rulers and ruled alike—were bound to doubt
whether people guilty of such violence were fit for self-government.
The Church feared for the future of religion and its hold on the
people; the faithful were determined not to be robbed of their strongly-
held beliefs; and the small farmer who tilled his own land distrusted
anything that came from the streets of Paris. Among German-speaking
Swiss, in fact, there was a deep-rooted aversion to all things French
and to foreign ideas in general. In French-speaking areas, however,
the reaction was different, and in parts of Vaud there were riots in
the early revolutionary years. In this confusing time, the Confederation was again beset by divisions and there was a widening split on
the issue of the country's neutrality. British agents were at work in
Switzerland, countering French influence and propaganda. The
country was under strain, pulled in two directions: France on the
one side, Britain and the old enemy Habsburg on the other. But the
official decision was to remain neutral; and because of Switzerland's
valuable strategic position, this suited France at the beginning of the
war. Before long, however, the picture changed.

To win over Switzerland, the French revolutionaries had to erode
its cherished ideals, supplant them with attractive new slogans or twist
them by skilful propaganda. They tried to persuade the Swiss that
tyranny must be fought in the name of William Tell. A bust of him
stood on the table of the clubroom of the Jacobin plotters, and at its
dedication ceremony someone said: "Fortunate the confederates who

have not forgotten that William Tell lived in their country. . . ." The cult of Tell was stepped up. There was even a mock Lord's Prayer invoking his name. It began : "William Tell, who art the founder of our freedom; thy name be hallowed in Switzerland; thy will be done also among us as it was done when thou wast victorious over thy tyrants." This prayer was circulated by Mengaud, the French chargé d'affaires in Basle, who secretly reported to Paris : "All is ready for an explosion." He had earlier softened up Holland; now he had laid his fuses in Switzerland. And soon the French burst into the Confederation with the cry : "Vive Guillaume Tell!"

The French made use of friends of the revolution among the Swiss. The most important was Peter Ochs, a gild-master in Basle. Ochs, born in France, became a willing tool of the revolution to which he was blindly devoted, contrasting it with what he called the "rotten Confederation" and "wretched privileges and puffed-up authority of our rulers." In Paris, a Swiss revolutionary club was formed, and its most prominent member was Frédéric César de la Harpe, a native of Vaud and a sincere and deeply patriotic man. His attitude to the Confederation had been moulded by bitter experience. His career in Switzerland had been blocked and he was mockingly reminded by a Bernese patrician that as a Vaudois he was a mere vassal. Russia showed greater sympathy, and Empress Catherine the Great appointed him as tutor to her grandson Alexander. The 30-year-old de la Harpe zealously endeavoured to bring the teachings of the Enlightenment to the future Tsar. Some ten years later, he appeared in Paris to prepare the ground for a French invasion of Switzerland by writing pamphlets in which he virtually invited the French to liberate Vaud. He believed that the deployment of French troops near the Jura mountains would be sufficient to frighten the Bernese into abdicating power in his native region. But the French exploited his petition for their own ends. To them it was important to gain control of the strategic passes in the central Alps and to get hold of Berne's well-filled treasure chests. In public, they concealed these two aims while loudly proclaiming a third : liberty for all the Swiss.

The old Confederation's most effective response to this assault would have been to show in good time that the Swiss were quite capable of looking after their own affairs and needed no foreign "liberators." But a different course was chosen. Zürich replied with force to reasonable demands from the country people of Stäfa on Lake Zürich who wanted a free constitution, tax relief and better education. This re-action of the rulers was a symptom of a general hardening of atti-tudes, and it brought protests from liberal-minded people. Pestalozzi, for one, was incensed by Zürich's reprisals; and the historian, Johannes von Müller, declared: "I know it is a bitter pill for the towns to sur-render their privileges for the well-being of the nation. My only answer is: there is no other way. Do what must be done, or others will do it for you!" The German physician J. G. Ebel, a devoted friend of the Swiss, whose Parisian patients included important politicians and who knew well what France was planning, gave a warning: "It is sheer madness to let foreigners gain the initiative in one's own country. The Swiss nation will face disaster if its leaders show such blindness and weakness." But blind they remained.

Delusions about the French were shattered when they marched into the Bernese Jura at the end of 1797. Then in the following January they used a blown-up frontier incident as a pretext for invading Vaud. Shortly beforehand, its people had proclaimed a new "République Lémanique," independent of Berne. But this did not dissuade France from invading; and indeed the Vaud capital, Lausanne, was forced to send 4,000 men to reinforce the uninvited French troops. It also had to buy its own freedom by granting the French a huge compul-sory loan—enough to dampen the people's revolutionary fervour.

The Bernese *Landvögte* now left the Vaudois castles. In Berne they found great indecision and a political see-saw between the peace and war parties. The leader of the war faction, the tough old chief magi-strate Niklaus Friedrich von Steiger, dug in his heels with the declara-tion: "You cannot escape the tiger's claws by patting them." But the appeasers argued that the French General Brune, whose forces were in Vaud, would listen to reason. They did not suspect that his smooth assurances were hiding his true aim—to carry on vague negotiations until his fellow-commander, General Schauenbourg, had occupied the Swiss positions at Bienne, north-west of Berne, and then to conquer the city by a swift assault from two directions.

Confusion grew among Bernese politicians and military men. The Great Council had appointed a resolute general in Karl Ludwig von Erlach, but first they did not give him enough troops and then tied his hands by negotiating with Brune. At the end of February

1798 he marched into the council chamber, accompanied by 72 officers, and demanded that either he be given full powers or dismissed.
The council agreed that he should launch an attack on 2 March at
dawn, but the order was countermanded when they received an ultim-
atum from Brune. This vacillation aroused further distrust among the
soldiers who felt they were expected to fight for a cause already betrayed. In any case it was difficult for 24,000 Bernese troops spread
out along a front of 125 miles to contain a two-pronged attack from
an enemy army of almost double their own strength. So on 2 March,
Berne's two old outposts, Fribourg and Solothurn, fell into enemy
hands. On 5 March the battle for Berne began, but despite individual acts of heroism and a vain appeal by General von Erlach to the
men of the local militia, the *Landsturm,* the French marched into the
city at half past two in the afternoon. The Great Council had already
dissolved itself. In the council chamber, one of Brune's secretaries
stuck a sheet of paper over the Bernese coat of arms on the chief magi-
strate's chair and wrote on it : "liberté—égalité." The state treasury
was raided, and even the bears, the heraldic beasts of Berne, the city
which had never yet seen enemy soldiers on its soil, were taken to
Paris. The age of Bernese aristocracy had come to an end.

The defeat proved to be the death-knell of the old Confederation.
In the crisis the confederates had failed to remain united.
There had been many fine expressions of goodwill five weeks earlier
during the last solemn oath-taking at the Diet in Aarau. But when
Berne was under attack the other cantons sent no more than 4,900
men to help, and most of these withdrew to protect their own lands,
abandoning Berne in the hope that they could still stem disaster nearer
home. The spirit of unity which had stood the test in the wars of
liberation had vanished.

7

The Dictates of France

O N 12 April 1798, little more than a month after the fall of Berne, cantonal representatives met again at Aarau, this time not to swear loyalty to the old Confederation but to bury it. At the dictates of France, they proclaimed the constitution of a new unitary state: the "One and Indivisible Helvetic Republic."

The new republic was one of several established by the French as they scattered their continental enemies of the first allied coalition and were left facing only Britain. In northern Italy, where Napoleon's triumphant campaign was crowned by the submission of Austria in the Treaty of Campo Formio, the conquered territories were grouped in the new Cisalpine Republic. It included the Valtellina area, detached from the Grisons on the ground that the Swiss had no right to hold a subject people. This pretext, elevated to the status of a principle, was a potential threat to Switzerland's frontiers elsewhere; and the situation looked particularly dangerous in another subject territory in the south, the Italian-speaking Ticino. Language, geography and the people's aspiration to freedom made the Ticino a tempting target for those who wanted to detach it from Switzerland. Unity with its Italian neighbour Lombardy and incorporation in the Cisalpine Republic were enticements offered. But when a band of armed Italians staged a sudden assault on Lugano in an effort to force the town to join Lombardy, the storm bells were rung and the Ticinese threw the Italians out with the battle-cry *Liberi e Svizzeri!* It is true that the people of the Ticino sought an end to their subject status, but their battle-cry showed they were determined to build their future as free and independent Swiss. In 1798 this clear assertion of loyalty to the political concept of Switzerland was the more remarkable since the whole of the country was at the mercy of the French, who controlled its mountain passes, imposed levies on its people and helped themselves to the wealth of its public treasuries.

Like the other dependent republics which France set up to protect her interests, the Helvetic Republic had a constitution imposed upon it, and one that showed scant regard for the country's customs, religion and political autonomy. Modelled on the new French constitution, it was put into force with the help of French bayonets. Bureaucratic uniformity was clamped on the Swiss. The very establishment of a unitary state marked the most flagrant break with traditional institutions. Once independent, even sovereign, cantons now totally lost their separate identities, and some of them even their old borders. The 23 cantons into which the new republic was divided became mere administrative districts under a system of prefects on the French pattern. The prefects had their district subordinates, and there were agents in the villages to represent the interests of the state. The executive of this bureaucracy consisted of a Directory of five, augmented at their discretion by a few other ministers. The Directory was elected by two legislative chambers, the Great Council and the Senate.

Under the new system there was also a Helvetic High Court; and the constitution provided for the separation of powers, as advocated 50 years earlier by Montesquieu in his desire to protect the rights of the individual from the abuse of authority. If the people's political traditions were ignored, they were at least now declared all equal in the eyes of the law. The complex structure of cantons and allies with its variety of subject relationships and class divisions was demolished. Freedom of religion and the press were established. In town and country, people were free to meet and form associations, and any group had the constitutional right to hand in petitions to the government. There were no restrictions on crafts and trades; property was declared inviolable; and feudal dues were to be swept away, a promise which before long was to arouse passionate argument in the countryside.

Despite the pledges of benefits and reform, the new constitution remained an artificial creation foisted on the people without consultation or vote, and as such it was given a very mixed reception. If the French and their supporters had expected nation-wide jubilation at the blessings of the revolution, they soon saw that the Swiss were much more reserved in their reaction than even their ordinary dispassionate temperament would warrant. Freedom trees were indeed raised in many parts of the country, and in the spring of 1798 the peasants still believed their burdens would melt like the winter's snow. But there were nevertheless misgivings in the countryside. Under the old regime, many peasants had enjoyed a great deal of self-rule within their own communities. Now they had suddenly been forced to give up this traditional status, as familiar to them as their own intimate cottages, and exchange it for citizenship within the spacious but impersonal structure of the new unified state.

In the towns, reaction to the new constitution also varied. Those traditionally under aristocratic government like Berne took to it much less than towns such as Zürich ruled by the guilds. In general, of course, the ruling class lamented the loss of its privileges. But the merchants hoped that the bold new political framework would enable trade to flourish without hindrance; while the workers, though not yet organised as a class, were clearly overjoyed to see the barriers to their advancement come down. The rise of the under-privileged to citizen status was applauded by men like Pestalozzi and the intellectual circles of Zürich, who hailed the establishment of the Helvetic Republic as a success for the ideas of the Enlightenment in Swiss politics. In Basle, the constitution found an obvious advocate in the revolutionary Peter Ochs, who had submitted proposals on it to Paris when drafting was going on early in the year. But Ochs was soon to realise that his handiwork was not being supported in the Swiss heartland.

Stubborn resistance came from the ancient *Landsgemeinde* cantons around Lake Lucerne. They were not impressed by the fact that Tell's image appeared on the seal of state. Naturally, the under-privileged inhabitants, the *Hintersaessen* and *Beisaessen,* were glad to be granted equal voting rights with the rest, but the great majority of the people of these cantons had been enjoying the rights of man under the Confederation for some 500 years. They had exercised their freedom in the popular assembly, and determined the fate of their little states by majority vote on a show of hands. Most important, all their problems had been thrashed out face to face with their own leaders. Now this vigorous, deep-rooted representation through *Landsgemeinden* was to be cut down and replaced under the new constitution by an ingenious mathematical concept providing for the election of one deputy for each 100 voters. One half of these deputies were to be eliminated by

lot; the others would go forward to elect the cantonal administrative
and judicial authorities, and to chose their canton's representatives in
the two legislative chambers.

Even when the new constitution was first proclaimed at Aarau,
deputies of the *Landsgemeinde* cantons had been absent, sparing
themselves the indignity of watching French grenadiers fire a salute
in honour of "Swiss independence." Now the Swiss mountain people
continued to express resentment at being forced into a constitutional
costume of Parisian design. They preferred their traditional Swiss
style; and their attitude was supported by the Church which de-
nounced the political fashions of Paris and the anti-clericalism of the
revolutionaries.

Resistance was not confined to verbal protest. The men of Glarus
and Schwyz took up arms when the Helvetic authorities asked the
French general Schauenbourg to impose the new order in their territories. The two cantons were defeated; and to punish them for their
opposition they were even deprived of their former names and reorganised into new cantons called Waldstätte, Linth and Säntis. In
September 1798, rebellion flared up again, this time in Nidwalden.
With heroic courage the tiny canton took on a vastly superior enemy.
Every farm was turned into a fortress, and Nidwalden did not give
in until it was crushed after appalling slaughter on both sides. Some
400 of its inhabitants, nearly one-third of them women and children,
were killed, while the French dead numbered more than 2,000.

After this tragedy, the Swiss orphans and homeless were cared for
by Pestalozzi, the great humanitarian who dedicated his life to children yet, despite everything, still saw hope in the new order. If the
Swiss fought resolutely to preserve their heritage, it must none the less
be recognised that the Helvetic Republic contained much that was
beneficial. Indeed, many of its innovations were later adopted by the
Swiss people and are still cherished privileges and liberties. The mistake
under the republic was the haste with which the new measures were
introduced without waiting for the right political climate. There were
also some basic errors of judgment, the main one being to abolish the
established cantonal structure which in effect meant the destruction
of the solid pillars on which the whole Swiss edifice rested. Another
dark shadow was cast over the land by the military alliance which the
new republic was forced to conclude with France, giving the French

the right to make free use of Swiss soldiers and territory. The result was that Switzerland, commanding the strategic Alpine passes, inevitably became a battlefield in the renewed struggle between France and her European opponents—the War of the Second Coalition.

In 1798, Napoleon decided to out-manoeuvre the British by launching a campaign in Egypt. His aim was to deal a blow to Britain's imperial power and her naval strength in the Mediterranean, but he suffered a shattering naval defeat at the hands of Nelson in the Battle of the Nile. Nelson's victory encouraged the Austrians and Russians to strike at France in Europe, and in one short campaign in the summer of 1799 France lost nearly all her gains in Italy. The Swiss were involved when the Russians, led by the tenacious veteran General Suvorov, invaded Italy and then, in a forced march over the St. Gotthard, advanced into Switzerland in an effort to link up with an allied army north of the Alps. But this northern army was defeated at Zürich by the commander of the French and Helvetic forces, General Masséna, while another French force at Altdorf blocked Suvorov's northward progress. The Russians were compelled to retreat across three mountain passes eastward to the Vorarlberg in Austria; this astounding operation cost Suvorov half his troops.

Switzerland as a battleground was in the pitiful position of all small buffer states that have been trampled over by foreign armies. The roar of guns in the Reuss and Linth valleys was followed by wholesale pillage, with peasants not only forced to hand over their draught animals but even to carry on their own backs the heavy loads of booty looted by the foreign troops. In this situation, the new system of government in the country seemed more than ever like a foreign imposition which had led to the sacrifice of Swiss interests, and all the misery and hardship were laid at the door of the new constitution. The Swiss seemed to forget their own political shortcomings and their failure in the past to organise a confederate army strong enough for the effective defence of the country.

By now, too, the peasants had become bitterly disillusioned over the promised reforms to free them from the oppressive burdens of compulsory labour, tithes and ground rents. The French at first gave an undertaking that these feudal dues would be abolished without compensation having to be paid to get rid of them; and the Swiss patriot and historian Johannes von Müller had seemed to be right in his prediction that such a pledge would win the people's allegiance. The Helvetic constitution, however, declared that compensation would have to be paid. This brought a fierce reaction from the peasants who felt that France's promise had been broken. After the outcry, a law abolishing the dues was passed. But in dispensing with compensation the government was depriving itself of a vital source of revenue at a time when it needed large sums to alleviate the burdens of war and rebuild the country. In the end, the only way out was the reintroduction of tithes and ground rents, causing even more bad blood. This inconsistency strengthened the critics in their view that the Helvetic legislators themselves did not know what they wanted. They produced ambitious blueprints, even brilliant ones, like the education plans of Philip Stapfer who envisaged primary education for all and a national university to crown a uniform state system of education. But most of the good intentions remained on paper, and all the while the Helvetic Republic was sinking into chaos.

Violent clashes of opinion developed, and two rival camps emerged : the centralists who held fast to the idea of a unitary state, and the federalists who saw salvation in a return to the old confederate system. For three years, there was anarchy and civil strife, with a complete lack of stability at the top and one unworkable constitution following another. When at last a fifth constitution was submitted to a referendum—the first to be held in Switzerland—only a fraction of the population bothered to go to the polls. The vote was : 72,000 in favour of the newly-proposed constitution, 92,000 expressly against it. But the vast body of non-voters were held to have approved it on the principle that silence signified assent.

Such was the situation as the Helvetic Republic drew to its end. Switzerland had been thrown into disarray by a system of government quite unsuited to its traditions. As things got worse it was only a question of time before there was bound to be an intervention by Napoleon Bonaparte, who had been First Consul of France since November 1799.

II NAPOLEON THE MEDIATOR

When the French had conquered the second coalition, and even Britain had temporarily withdrawn from the struggle, the First Consul turned his attention to Switzerland. "You," he told the Swiss, "have been offering a sad spectacle. Swiss blood has been shed by Swiss hands. For three years you have been quarrelling without understanding one another. If you are left any longer to yourselves you will go on killing one another for three more years."

Napoleon had no intention of leaving the Swiss to themselves. By the end of 1802, he had summoned representatives of the Senate and all the cantons to Paris and a *Helvetic consulta* was at work on a new Swiss constitution. An address he made to the *consulta* was a masterpiece of political psychology. It was Napoleon speaking as a Corsican, as a man of understanding. "I speak to you," he said, "as if I were Swiss myself. Federation is of exceptional importance to small countries. I myself was born in a land of mountains and I understand how mountain people think." He referred with particular respect to the *Landsgemeinde* cantons which, he said, distinguished the Swiss constitutionally from all other countries and gave them their individual character in the eyes of the world.

The deliberations of the *consulta,* under the eyes of Napoleon, resulted in the Act of Mediation of 19 February 1803. It reflected what the First Consul had said about federation, producing a constitutional solution which was more like the old Confederation than the unitary state which had just fallen in ruins. Significantly, it dealt with the constitutional position of each individual canton before setting out the federal details. Under the Mediation Act, the Helvetic Republic was replaced by a Confederation of 19 cantons. The former 13 cantons, which were virtually unchanged, were joined by six new ones : St. Gallen, Aargau, the Grisons, Thurgau, the Ticino and Vaud. These six were formed from the old allied and subject territories which had been abolished. The Confederation did not include Neuchâtel, the Valais or Geneva, which was seized by France during the revolution; but in general Swiss territory remained intact. The *Landsgemeinde* cantons had their democratic rights and sovereignty almost entirely restored, and the six new cantons became representative democracies. But Napoleon's revolutionary background was not strongly reflected in the provisions for the seven city cantons, where a franchise based on very high property qualifications revived the predominance of the rich towns over the poorer rural areas and tended to preserve the power of the aristocracy. This was so although the

Mediation Act banned all privilege based on family and residence and incorporated some of the egalitarian principles of the French revolution.

Under the Mediation Act, the Diet had only limited powers and there was no permanent capital. In the Diet, cantons with more than 100,000 population had two representatives, the rest one. Their authority was weak, but the old obstructive requirement of unanimity was removed, the support of three-quarters of the cantons being sufficient for decisions on peace and war and for the conclusion of treaties. The Diet assembled normally only once a year, holding its meetings alternately in six so-called director-cantons, three Protestant and three Catholic : Zürich, Basle, Berne, Lucerne, Fribourg and Solothurn. The supreme authority of the Confederation was symbolised in the chief magistrate of the year's director-canton who assumed the title of *Landamman* of Switzerland, presiding over the Diet and representing the Confederation at home and abroad. This appointment was a departure from Swiss tradition, and for Napoleon it had the advantage that there was a single representative of Switzerland at hand on whom he could put pressure.

The Act of Mediation was beneficial in that it recognised that a centralised form of government had not been the best for Swiss conditions. It also settled the civil strife which had been dividing the country. But Napoleon intended to see that French interests were the paramount consideration. Above all, he made it clear that he wanted manpower for his army. He sent General Ney to the opening of the new Diet, and the French general announced that he was authorised to conclude a defence pact and a military capitulation giving Napoleon the right to demand the services of 16,000 Swiss troops through voluntary enlistment. Completely disregarding any principle of Swiss neutrality, Napoleon also laid it down that Switzerland should be allowed to conclude similar agreements only with pro-French powers. Neutrality, as Napoleon himself remarked, meant nothing to him. The Diet took General Ney's announcement as an order : it could do little else. How completely Switzerland was at Napoleon's mercy was seen when he suggested on one occasion that he might take it over altogether. When it suited him in 1810, he incorporated the Valais into his Empire, because of its new and vital road linking France and Italy.

Another serious blow to Switzerland came from the blockade which Napoleon imposed under his Continental System in an effort to strangle Britain's trade and establish French economic supremacy in Europe. The Swiss textile industry was hit especially hard because it was prevented by the blockade from importing essential raw materials. There was massive unemployment, and in eastern Switzerland 20,000 weavers' families were starving. Amidst these pressures and problems, the Diet managed to take some action to tackle the economic situation, approving an ingenious emergency plan to improve the river Linth. In the past, the river had silted up, causing serious flooding in the area which became a vast disease-bearing marshland. Under the new scheme, the river was diverted into the Walensee, offering better opportunities for shipping and draining the lowlands of Glarus so that they became suitable for farming.

In economic matters as in government, the mark of Napoleon was left on Switzerland for good or ill. The Emperor of the French, as he proclaimed himself in 1804, cast his shadow across the Swiss people as once the Holy Roman Empire had done. But now the pretensions of the Holy Roman Emperors had finally collapsed after a thousand years, swept away in the fury of the times. The dream of Empire was Napoleon's, and it was to be his undoing, despite his immense achievements and the conquests that at the height of his power made him dominant in nearly every corner of Europe. The ferocity of his ambition drove Europe on at a breakneck speed, by a process of action and reaction, and along with the revolutionary changes went the suffering. Yet, at a time when war swept across the Continent, Switzerland could count one blessing : for year there were no battles on its soil. Nevertheless, the people found conditions under the Act of Mediation the harder to endure the more arrogant Napoleon's behaviour towards them became. Service with the French forces lost its appeal, and recruits had to be procured by compulsion for Napoleon's desperate gamble of 1812—the invasion of Russia.

The Grand Army that set out in June 1812 numbered some half a million men, but no more than half of them were French. The rest were drawn from many other parts of Europe. In their ranks were 9,000 Swiss, who played a courageous part in covering the Grand Army's westward retreat from Moscow across the Berezina. The losses were catastrophic. It is estimated that only about a tenth of the Swiss troops survived, and the story was similar in the other contingents. Yet this tremendous set-back for France was followed by another of Napoleon's big achievements in military organisation. Within a year he had rebuilt his army to confront the allies again. But at Leipzig, in the Battle of the Nations of October 1813, he suffered a crushing blow, and this time the French retreat was to be followed by a triumphant allied drive on Paris. In the process, nearly 100,000 troops under Austrian command invaded Switzerland across the Rhine and then marched on into France in an attempt to outflank the Napoleonic forces. Resistance by the small Swiss frontier units was useless and they had to be withdrawn.

After Napoleon's banishment to Elba and his subsequent escape, Switzerland had to give up any idea of neutrality in the face of the overwhelming allied pressure to rally all support for the final over-throw of Napoleon. His amazing last Hundred Days as Emperor in Paris ended on the field of Waterloo on 18 June 1815. Then came imprisonment on St. Helena, where he died in 1821. By that time Europe had been reshaped under the pressures of reaction after a quarter of a century of revolution and war.

Restoration in France and reorganisation in Europe generally had begun well before Napoleon's alarming reappearance. The Bourbons had been put back on the French throne in the person of Louis XVIII; at a Paris peace conference the allies had concluded a treaty with France; and the brilliant Congress of Vienna had met to redraw the map of Europe. It was here that Switzerland's borders were de-termined. The inclusion of Geneva, Neuchâtel and the Valais brought the number of cantons to 22, as at present, though Valtellina* was annexed to the kingdom of Lombardo-Venetia which was held by the Austrian Emperor. Another important aim of Swiss policy was achieved at the second Paris peace conference, after the final fall of Napoleon. Largely thanks to the patient work of the Genevese nego-tiator Pictet de Rochemont, Switzerland's wish to have its neutrality recognised in international law was fulfilled. On 20 November 1815, the five big powers—Britain, Austria, France, Prussia and Russia together with Portugal—issued a declaration on the subject. They

---

* In 1859, Valtellina, like the rest of Lombardy, became part of the Italian kingdom; and today the whole valley, except Poschiavo (Puschlav) which is part of the Grisons, belongs to Italy.

guaranteed the integrity and inviolability of Swiss territory and recognised its permanent neutrality. They stated explicitly that "the neutrality and integrity of Switzerland and its independence from any foreign influence are in the true interests of all European states."

Swiss neutrality was neither an act of charity by the great powers nor their invention. They were confirming a 300-year-old principle of Swiss foreign policy which has since been rigorously observed. For the last 150 years and more, no foreign army has invaded Switzerland and no Swiss army has crossed the frontiers in pursuit of territorial gain. In the past, the existence of two powerful faiths within Switzerland would have endangered the Confederation's survival if it had become involved in the religious wars of Europe; now in the age of nationalism, it was the multi-lingual character of the republic that counselled a cautious policy. But of supreme importance was the country's common will for law, order and peace. The Swiss wanted to make their neutrality permanent. It was not to be just a passive attitude, as sometimes in the past, but an active and essential element in their whole approach to foreign policy. They were prepared to defend it, and from 1815 onwards they began to strengthen their army. But neutrality did not mean that Switzerland intended to close its eyes to the affairs of the world or to disclaim responsibility for its share in them. Half a century later neutrality was given concrete meaning when the land of the White Cross became the centre from which the Red Cross operated to bring relief to those who suffered in war.

Johann Heinrich Pestalozzi (1746–1827), the great Swiss educationist whose work for children influenced attitudes far beyond his own country.

The modern city of Geneva, centre of trade,
industry, culture and international
organizations.

8

Reaction and Revolt: 1815–1848

I RESTORATION

NAPOLEON'S ACT of Mediation did not survive his downfall and Switzerland needed a new fundamental law by which to organise its life. After long and stormy discussions, a Federal Pact on the constitutional future was hammered out by the Swiss themselves at the Diet in Zürich in September 1815. In essence the Federal Pact meant the triumph of reaction, the restoration of a conservative regime, a weak and ineffectual Diet and the dominance of federalism—all of which reflected the spirit of the post-Napoleonic era not only in Switzerland but among the victorious allies themselves.

After the violence of the French Revolution and the Napoleonic conquests, after all the beating of drums and roar of battle, a great nostalgia and a longing for peace settled over the continent. There was a widespread feeling that if only the leaders would ensure permanent peace, putting an end to the fighting, bloodshed and hardship that had seemed endless in the past 25 years, they were welcome to run the affairs of state in their own way. Many people came to look on the times of the *ancien régime* as the good old days, and in this atmosphere politics reverted to pre-revolutionary style. Monarchy was again supreme : the great watchword was "restoration." This term, used to describe the whole period, was drawn from the title of a Swiss counter-revolutionary work, Karl Ludwig von Haller's *Restauration der Staatswissenschaft*. Haller, a Bernese patrician, expounded the conservative view of the state, strongly disputing Rousseau's doctrines. Haller argued that after legitimate rulers had been reinstated, a legitimate theory of government, too, must be restored. In particular, he opposed Rousseau's argument that all men are equal by nature and that, as a result of a social contract, governments rule by virtue of the power given to them by the people. For Haller, it was both in accordance with the laws of nature and God's will that the strong should rule the weak. In his view, government by the more powerful as of right ought to be the basic idea of the state. This was the spirit displayed at the Congress of Vienna by the Austrian Chancellor Metternich whose name came to signify the essence of conservative and anti-revolutionary rule. In the 30 years and more that Metternich dominated the political scene, until the European revolutions of 1848, he sought to preserve aristocratic control from what he considered the pretentious claims of the radical middle classes.

Switzerland could not escape the spirit of reaction, but fortunately it proved impossible to turn the wheel of history right back to the conditions before 1798. Restoration did indeed mean a revival of the old loosely-knit Confederation, but if aristocrats imagined they could plunge some cantons back into an antiquated subject status they were soon made to face reality. The cantons that had been formed from the old subject territories during the Napoleonic era resisted such a retrograde step, and they were supported by the commonsense of the majority of Switzerland's population. The Federal Pact of 1815 followed the example of the Mediation Act in refusing to permit subject districts, though the towns did in fact maintain their supremacy over the rural areas for years to come. Berne, for example, accepted no more than 99 representatives of its surrounding territory into its ruling Council of Two Hundred, although the rural population was at least 30 times larger than that of the city.

The Federal Pact reduced the powers of central government and ensured that the cantons once again enjoyed almost complete sovereignty. In contrast to the arrangement under the Act of Mediation, each canton had an equal vote in the Diet irrespective of the size of its population. Questions of peace and war and the conclusion of treaties could be decided by a three-quarter majority of the representatives who voted on instructions from their cantons. In all other matters an absolute majority was sufficient, but such matters were usually of little significance in view of the power of the individual cantons to order their own affairs. They were even given the right to conclude military capitulations with foreign countries as long as such arrangements to provide mercenaries conflicted neither with existing alliances nor with the Swiss constitution. In domestic affairs, the Federal Pact contained one important restriction on cantonal sovereignty which was to take on crucial significance in the years ahead: it prohibited internal alliances between individual cantons which might be harmful to the others or to the Confederation as a whole. The cantons were also called upon to make some contribution to the federal treasury, in proportion to their population. As for the army, it comprised less than 33,000 men to begin with; but it was soon doubled in size, and this was important if neutrality was ever to be effectively defended.

These cautious restraints on the power of the cantons did not alter the fact that central government remained abysmally weak. Its only permanent officials were a chancellor and a secretary; and for a long time to come the entire confederate secretariat could be numbered on the fingers of one hand. They were a kind of travelling troupe which changed headquarters every two years, moving between the director-cantons which now numbered three: Zürich, Berne and Lucerne. The whole secretariat was transported in a single carriage, and on one ludicrous occasion this confederate state coach literally got stuck in the snow near the Reuss bridge at Mellingen—a symbol of the impotence of central government. Yet how could this state of affairs be changed when the Federal Pact intentionally contained no clause providing for lawful amendment of the constitution?

Politically weak though it was, the new Swiss Confederation entered into a period of economic recovery. Alpine roads were built, promoting traffic across the St. Gotthard and other passes. In the lowlands, the waterways took on even more importance with the appearance of steamships on the big lakes. Industry, still in its infancy, took to steam power with some hesitation; nevertheless Switzerland managed not to be left hopelessly behind by Britain with its rich coal deposits. The Swiss owed this success in part to the ingenuity of their entrepreneurs and the diligence of their workers, but above all to the way they harnessed their country's vast potential in water power. Factories were built along fast-flowing rivers and Glarus at that time became the most highly industrialised region. Water power was decisive for the establishment of most Swiss industry in rural areas, a tradition which has continued to the present time and meant that Switzerland developed neither huge urban conglomerations nor an industrial proletariat on the English model. The expanding economy provided jobs for the men who were no longer making a living out of mercenary service abroad. But the majority of the working people also kept a cow and some sheep and carried on a little farming on the side. Without this supply from their own plots and fields the Swiss would have suffered even more bitterly in the famine years of 1816–17, when the French stranglehold on Swiss imports and exports was disastrously aggravated by crop failures.

Economic progress could have been faster had it not been for the isolationist policy of the individual cantons, which imposed absurd trade and customs barriers against each other. Each year about ten new turnpikes went up, and in 1823 the federal tariff inspector listed more than 400 places where traders had to halt and pay customs duties, safe conduct and convoy fees, bridge tolls and the like. Between Ragaz and Rapperswil, for example, merchants had to stop no less than 28 times in about 30 miles to pay dues. Small wonder that it was quicker and cheaper to transport goods from Basle to Geneva by-passing Switzerland altogether!

The weakness of Switzerland under the Federal Pact was reflected above all in the country's foreign relations. Tsar Alexander's anti-liberal Holy Alliance of continental autocracies, which nearly all European powers were asked to join, was an oppressive instrument in Metternich's hands. It pervaded the domestic affairs of European states and conflicted with the popular aspirations that were developing. Britain, with her essentially liberal policy, refused to join. As to Switzerland, which ultimately had to become a member, its entire political life was affected by Metternich's surveillance. Foreign snoopers kept an eye on everything, Swiss newspapers were scrutinised with suspicion, and the powers of the Holy Alliance demanded that Switzerland hand over refugees who had fled there in search of a more liberal climate. Under threats and pressure from Vienna, Switzerland was compelled in 1823 to agree to the Press and Aliens Conclusum whereby it had to shackle its press completely and deny asylum to political refugees. Not long before, the Swiss were at Napoleon's mercy; now they had to do Metternich's bidding.

II REGENERATION

As the Swiss people found the suppression of their liberty increasingly humiliating, the first signs of a liberal revolt emerged, at the heart of

which were the young and the educated. Students who had passed
through German universities were inspired by Goethe's view of life,
Kant's sense of moral responsibility, and the stirring idealism of Schiller, whose passionate assertion of liberty made his play, *Wilhelm Tell,*
Switzerland's national drama. In this climate of ideas, eyes turned
towards the sufferings of Greece, and dedicated philhellenists rallied
to the support of the Greeks in their struggle for freedom during the
1820s. The ancient ideals of Switzerland's own history of struggle
became a fresh source of inspiration, encouraging the revival of the
Helvetic Society, whose spiritual leader, the Swiss philosopher Paul
Vital Troxler, untiringly reminded its members of the principles of
the original Confederation.

It was not only the intellectuals, either, who were thirsting for
liberty and national unity. An outlet for this revival of the national
spirit was found in the widespread formation of community groups
such as choral societies, associations of marksmen, and students' clubs.
They sprang up all over the country, holding meetings and festivals
which were made the occasion for proclamations of faith in the ideal
of a strong, united Confederation.

The ordinary people, as well as the intellectuals, found the muzzle
of censorship intolerable. The first to cast it off was the *Landsgemeinde*
of Appenzell, where the *Appenzeller Zeitung* became the champion
of liberalism. In Zürich, the demand for a free press was voiced in
a fiery speech by a member of the city's Great Council, Paul Usteri.
Every country, he declared, needs an enlightened public opinion to
keep a check on government; in a republic, in particular, everyone
must take part in public affairs, and the best way of doing so is
through a free press. Usteri's liberal speech struck home: in due
course Zürich abolished its censorship which back in the 16th and
17th centuries had led to 74 death sentences for defamation of authority and other offences. In 1829, the Confederation as a whole rid
itself of the shackles of the Press and Aliens Conclusum, and the
result was not, as pessimists had predicted, a flood of lies and slander.
Quite the contrary: a responsible, free press helped to train the
people to respect and spread truth in the coming age of liberal
democracy.

Along with the movement for national unity and political liberty,
there went demands for economic integration and a break-down of

the barriers to the growth of trade and industry in the Confederation. Social aspirations and unrest also played their part in changing the economic climate, with the rise of the middle class and the effects of the factory system on working people. Cottage workers with their spinning wheels at home were threatened with a loss of earnings from the day that the so-called king of the spinners, Heinrich Kunz, set up a cotton mill at Uster in the canton of Zürich. The machine was the enemy; the mill was hell; reaction against both was fierce in the unsettled conditions of the time. And the workers of Uster, who believed like the English Luddites that they could halt industrial progress, set the factory on fire.

All these social, political and economic forces provided the background and impetus for the country's "regeneration," as the movement for change in this period came to be known. As before, the spark which eventually started the blaze came from France, where the prominent advocates of the new liberal ideas included a native of Vaud, Benjamin Constant. Popular impatience with absolutist rule in France exploded in July 1830 when King Charles X issued decrees which limited the freedom of the press and were regarded as a severe threat to the constitution. The fate of France was once more decided on the barricades; the king was driven from his throne and succeeded by the bourgeois monarch, Louis Philippe of Orléans.

The July revolution fired the Swiss with excitement. In canton after canton the cry went up for new liberal constitutions which would express the will of the people, thousands of whom were rallying to public meetings to demand a bigger say in political affairs. The most dramatic demonstration was held at Uster, where 10,000 rural people gathered in November 1830 to insist on increased representation on Zürich's Great Council. The country population refused any longer to tolerate a situation in which the city with 15,000 inhabitants sent 130 representatives while a mere 82 were allowed to speak for the rural districts, which had a population 20 times as large. The Memorial of Uster, the document submitted to the burgomaster of Zürich, demanded that two-thirds of the members of the council should be rural representatives, and that the council should hold its meetings in public. The Memorial also called for lower taxes and better schools, and voiced the local complaints about the use of machinery in the cotton industry. The council gave way to the main political demands, and in March 1831 an overwhelming majority of the people of Zürich approved a new constitution. It typified representative democracy, with the people's rights held in trust by a representative institution, the cantonal Great Council, which was to embody their sovereign will.

The regeneration movement triumphed in all the cantons of the Swiss plateau from Lake Constance to Lake Geneva. Although not a single shot was fired in this self-disciplined liberal revolution, which embraced two-thirds of the Swiss population, some cantonal governments agreed to reforms only after they had been confronted by the persuasive power of mass meetings and, at Aarau and Lausanne, the sight of demonstrators on the march to the administrative capitals. It was a rebellion of the villages, under the leadership of the little country towns whose lawyers, pastors, teachers and doctors felt underprivileged in comparison with the people of the cities. In the cantons which accepted reforms—and they were the most important parts of the Confederation—the rebellion secured the main aims of the Liberals: the sovereignty of the people, representative democracy, open meetings of the Great Councils and local assemblies, freedom of speech, association and settlement. Even where the new cantonal constitutions did not fully satisfy the principle of complete equality before the law and universal suffrage, the agreed political liberties were at least spelt out and guaranteed.

Reform had come first in the cantons, in accordance with Switzerland's confederate structure, but the Liberals were pressing for the new concepts to be applied on a national level as well. The Diet instructed a commission to produce a draft federal constitution based on the ideas of Count Pellegrino Rossi of Geneva. His proposals did not envisage a drastic break with the past but involved supplementing the Diet by a Federal Council of five and a Federal Court. This was not enough for the innovators and too much for the traditionalists. In general, the proposals had little public appeal; and not even liberal Lucerne, which was nominated as federal capital, was prepared to accept them.

This was a setback for the regeneration movement, which was now up against the old divisions in the Confederation and in danger from a reaction against liberalism. The reforms had been introduced more or less smoothly in many populous cantons, seven of which grouped themselves in the so-called *Siebenerkonkordat*; but in some places regeneration was blocked, notably in Neuchâtel, Schwyz and Basle, with their stubbornly defended conservative traditions. In Neuchâtel, with its entrenched aristocracy, there were numerous immigrants whose liberal and revolutionary ideas appealed to a growing section of the population and strengthened the newly-founded Republican party. The aristocratic families would have nothing to do with these innovations, however, and the majority of citizens were loyal to the government, with the result that in 1831 two Republican attempts to seize power failed.

In Schwyz, the people of outlying areas more recently added to the canton were refused equal status by those who enjoyed ancient traditional rights. The traditionalists leaned for support on the League of Sarnen, a protective grouping whose members, apart from Schwyz, were the Valais, Neuchâtel and Basle. The Diet had the greatest difficulty in preventing a territorial split in Schwyz, such as was to occur in Basle where the conflict between town and country was particularly bitter. The bourgeoisie and artisans of Basle, burdened by a heavy load of taxation, refused to agree to adequate numerical representation of the rural districts on the Great Council. In an armed clash between the two sides the townspeople were defeated, but rather than accept "peasants' rule" they settled for the establishment in 1833 of two separate half-cantons: Basle-Town comprising the city and its suburbs, and Basle-Country which included the rest of the canton.

Regeneration was also confronted with pressures from outside. The movement had been followed with growing misgivings by the continental powers, for it was attracting champions of liberty from everywhere and Swiss territory was a haven for refugees. Despite all its problems, Switzerland was a republic inspiring liberal hopes in a Europe of monarchies still set on resisting change. It was from Switzerland in 1834 that the Italian nationalist and revolutionary Giuseppe Mazzini sailed across Lake Geneva, accompanied by Italian compatriots, Germans and Poles, to invade Savoy and proclaim an Italian republic. The ambitious enterprise failed miserably; and so at this time did that of another prominent exile in Switzerland, Louis Napoleon. His aim was to inherit his uncle's once-glorious throne in France by overthrowing Louis Philippe; and he had been plotting to this end at Arenenberg in the canton of Thurgau, where he was made an honorary citizen after he and his mother had found asylum there. When he failed in an attempt to seize Strasbourg in 1836, he was arrested by the French and deported to America. Later he made his way back to Arenenberg, where his mother was dying. The French demanded his extradition, sent 25,000 men to the border, and threatened to invade Switzerland. The Swiss armed themselves for battle, but were spared the encounter by Louis Napoleon's voluntary departure for England in 1838.

In none of these incidents had the Confederation shown itself capable of conducting a strong internal or foreign policy. Intelligent and far-sighted Liberals realised that for unity and democracy to succeed the people would have to be thoroughly trained and educated in self-government and in the exercise of political freedom. From now on the school, jointly with Church and home, was entrusted with the task of instructing the younger generation in civic responsibility. At last Pestalozzi's educational ideas were coming to be fulfilled. The foundations were laid for primary schools in which the poor could have their children educated free, and which the rich found preferable to private tuition. The Swiss primary school became a training ground for democracy. In the field of higher education, Switzerland's main university, at Zürich, was opened in 1833, and a teachers' training college was also established in the canton.

The leading role of the state in matters of education, however, was not gladly accepted by the Church which was particularly perturbed by the growing influence of the Radicals, as the left wing of the Liberals came to be known. The Radicals were strongly anti-clerical and determined to press far more vigorously than the moderate Liberals for democracy and social reform. Educational expansion had brought many foreign university professors and lecturers to Switzerland, and the Radicals attracted violent opposition from the Church when they secured the appointment at Zürich university of the German theologian David Friedrich Strauss whom orthodox believers regarded as a freethinker. The Church's views were backed by many factory owners for their own reasons: they were up in arms over the progressive teachers' objection to the employment of children for night work in the factories. Faced with this powerful opposition from Church and industry, the Radical government had to yield to pressure and retire Strauss before he could even take up his post. After this trial of strength in which their Church had triumphed, thousands of country folk marched on Zürich, singing hymns as they went. The government wilted before this chorus of rebellion, and in September 1839 it was replaced. Zürich, a pioneer of liberalism, had joined the conservative camp.

III   THE SONDERBUND WAR

Reaction in Zürich was the signal for renewed clerical opposition to liberalism elsewhere; and religious divisions sharpened. In times past such divisions had endangered the Confederation, and now again they were to lead to civil war.

In 1841 the constitution of Aargau, a religiously mixed canton, was changed to meet Liberal demands that the Protestants should have more representatives on the Great Council than the less numerous Catholics. The Catholics protested and took up arms. Their revolt was quickly put down by the Aargau government; but that was not the end of the affair. The Radicals and their supporters believed that the monasteries were implicated in the rising, and eight monasteries were accordingly dissolved by the Great Council. This caused uproar among the Catholics and brought protests from several cantons. Aargau was held to have violated the Federal Pact of 1815, which had guaranteed the continued existence of the monasteries. Appeals along these lines were made to the Diet, which was placed in a difficult and embarrassing position. It finally settled by a narrow majority for a compromise solution after Aargau had allowed the reopening of four nunneries clearly not involved in the Catholic rising. The compromise satisfied no one, and some Catholics were now even contemplating political separation from the Protestant cantons.

The dissolution of the Aargau monasteries reopened the old sores of the religious wars. Lucerne was another centre of conflict. In 1841 it moved away from liberalism and introduced a conservative-clerical constitution. This involved an extension of democratic rights in so far as it gave the rural population a bigger say in the canton's affairs. However, it also entrusted the Church with control of education; and its prime mover, a loyal and popular churchman, Josef Leu von Ebersol, wanted the Jesuits to take charge of higher educational institutions as they had already done in Schwyz. He and his supporters were strongly advised against this course, even by Metternich. But a motion in the Diet to have the Jesuits expelled from Switzerland was defeated, and the Great Council of Lucerne decided to go ahead with the plan to invite them. This decision by the director-canton of the time was regarded as a provocation by the Radicals, and by most Protestants.

Lucerne had acted within its rights under the Federal Pact and legally its decision could not be challenged. But in the eyes of the Radicals and many others the Jesuits were militant reactionaries, the enemies of a free, progressive society. Lucerne's action therefore turned out to have been a major political mistake, with repercussions in the whole of Switzerland. The Radicals organised groups of volunteers— the *Freischärler*—to bring down the cantonal government. But two armed expeditions of men from various parts of the country ended in humiliation and many of the volunteers were thrown into prison. One of them, a down-and-out peasant, later took revenge by assassinating Josef Leu von Ebersol in a bedroom at his home.

The *Freischärler* had breached the peace of the land and the situation was bordering on anarchy. The Catholic cantons were getting more and more alarmed. Finally in 1845 Lucerne, Uri, Schwyz, Unterwalden, Zug, Fribourg and the Valais concluded a separate pact for self-defence—the *Sonderbund*. They kept it secret until the following year, but immediately began political talks with foreign powers. Months earlier even, the burgomaster of Lucerne and chairman of the Sonderbund's war council, Siegwart-Müller, had already asked Metternich for help. He finally went as far as handing a memorandum to the Austrian ambassador which contained proposals for the Bernese Oberland to be split up between Unterwalden and the Valais and for the Catholic districts of Aargau to be incorporated in the canton of Lucerne. In this way, Siegwart-Müller suggested, a wedge could be driven between Berne and Zürich, and an easier link forged between the Catholic cantons of central Switzerland and the Black Forest, the native region of his family.

When the secret pact was revealed, grave doubts arose all over Switzerland about this potentially disastrous and treasonable league. Did not the Sonderbund conflict with article VI of the Federal Pact which prohibited "alliances between individual cantons prejudicial to the Confederation as a whole or to the rights of other cantons?" More and more cantons were of the opinion that the Sonderbund constituted a violation of the Pact, and the issue had to be dealt with by the Diet. By then Zürich had returned to the progressive fold, and a coup d'état had brought the Radicals to power in Geneva. In general, the Radicals were gaining ground over the more cautious Liberals and by 1847 half the cantons had taken sides against the Sonderbund. The interest now focused on St. Gallen, where decisive elections were held in the spring of that year. The result brought the canton into the Radical camp in the Diet, and this produced an absolute majority in favour of action against the Sonderbund. The Diet declared the alliance incompatible with the Federal Pact, and called for its dissolution. It also demanded the expulsion of the Jesuits from Switzerland and the replacement of the rigid Federal Pact by a more democratic constitution.

The Sonderbund reacted by preparing for war and again urgently appealed for help from abroad. It even conferred the initial military command on a foreigner. Ultimately, it was a Protestant from the Grisons who became commander-in-chief: Johann Ulrich von Salis-Soglio. In the second half of October 1847, the Diet assembled in Berne, that year's director-canton. The meeting was chaired by Ulrich Ochsenbein, a former leader of the *Freischärler* who was now president of the Bernese government and as such also president of the Confederation. The arguments put forward by him and the other Radicals carried the day. The Diet decided to dissolve the Sonderbund by force of arms. When the meeting ended, the representatives of the Sonderbund cantons left the hall without a word. The silence was broken only by the drum roll of the guard in a final military salute to the departing confederates. The Diet's decision meant civil war.

A protracted struggle would have been disastrous for the Confederation, perhaps tearing it apart and leaving it at the big powers' mercy. Once war began it was vital for the Diet to secure quick victory with the least possible bloodshed. The Confederation showed political wisdom in selecting the sixty-year-old Guillaume Henri Dufour of Geneva as its military leader. General Dufour was no Radical: in politics he was conservative. But he was widely admired as a patriot, a man of unblemished character, and a humanitarian whose orders to his troops reflected his concern to spare the civilian population. He had received training in Paris, served in the Napoleonic wars, and afterwards was director of the military academy at Thun in the canton of Berne. As a celebrated cartographer, he had detailed knowledge of the terrain over which the civil war was to be fought.

The course of the war against the Sonderbund was determined by Dufour's strategy, which was vastly superior to that of his opponent. Salis-Soglio was handicapped by disunity between the Sonderbund's war council and the army command and by difficult communications over the widely separated areas under his control. When fighting began in November 1847 Dufour decided to ignore the Valais for the time being and concentrate his forces first against Fribourg and then Lucerne. He neither allowed himself to be deflected by enemy raids from Uri southwards across the St. Gotthard nor by an invasion of Aargau territory. His strategy brought quick results.

Fribourg was forced to capitulate on 14 November. A week later Zug surrendered, to be followed two days after that by Lucerne. Then the other members of the Sonderbund also abandoned the struggle as hopeless. Dufour had brought his campaign to a successful conclusion within just over three weeks, and the cost in human life was low. Seventy-eight federal troops were killed, and the Sonderbund losses were only half that number.

Dufour's masterly strategy had ended the war before France, Austria and Prussia could do anything to rescue the Sonderbund, though they would certainly have liked to prevent its collapse. In summer 1847 the French ambassador had threatened armed inter-vention, to which the Swiss President, Ochsenbein, proudly retorted that if the European monarchies wanted to take on such a risky gamble, Switzerland was ready to play their game. Their negotiations on how to respond to increasingly urgent appeals from the Sonder-bund were protracted, however, largely because of British policy. Lord Palmerston, and British public opinion in general, showed understand-ing and sympathy for liberalism in Europe; and Palmerston skilfully managed to delay intervention by the other powers long enough for their eventual offer of mediation in the war to become meaningless. By the time the Swiss Diet received notes from France, Austria and Prussia in early December 1847, the Sonderbund had been dissolved. The Diet replied somewhat sarcastically that while it appreciated the powers' kind concern, an offer of mediation presupposed a state of war which no longer existed.

France, Austria and Prussia made one more attempt to frustrate the reform of the Swiss constitution by asserting that the Federal Pact of 1815 could be amended only with the approval of all 22 cantons. But the burgomaster of Zürich, Jonas Furrer, who was to play a leading part in shaping the new constitution, reminded them of their own declaration in 1815 that it would be in Europe's interest if neutral Switzerland remained independent of any foreign influence. This turned out to be the final answer. Within a few weeks, the three powers would have found it very difficult to exert any effective pressure on Switzerland. By then they had enough troubles of their own at home. The revolutionary upheavals of 1848 had begun; and in the words of Madame Metternich it was as if "all hell had broken loose."

IV THE YEAR OF RENEWAL

The year 1848 produced a chain-reaction in the affairs of Europe, a dramatic demonstration of the links connecting its peoples. Revolution flashed from country to country, striking down Metternich and Louis Philippe and leaving other rulers numb with the shock of it. In February, the barricades went up in Paris, the king abdicated, and a new provisional government of Liberals and Socialists was set up, pledged to social reform and work for all. The events in France were once again the signal for risings elsewhere in the name of liberty and nationalism. In March, demonstrations broke out in Vienna, Metternich was overthrown, and the Austrian Empire faced the revolt of nationalists in Hungary and Bohemia. National unity was the slogan of rebellion in the two great divided countries, Italy and Germany. In Berlin, riots and barricades brought a revolutionary crisis for King Frederick William IV of Prussia, who had remarked of the Liberals in Switzerland: "The triumph of that pack will infect Germany, Italy and France."

The revolutionary mood, inspired by France, was certainly infectious. The great nations around Switzerland were all caught up in it. In the early months of 1848 it seemed that in one bold stroke they would accomplish the aims of liberty and unity towards which the Swiss had long been struggling. But then the movement went into reverse. In France, the new leaders had promised more than they could fulfil, the national-workshops plan to relieve unemployment proved a total failure, and by June Paris was gripped by insurrection. After the bloody fighting involved in its suppression, the French people as a whole yearned for firm government. The way was open for Louis Napoleon to raise the Bonaparte standard. In December he was elected President of the Second Republic. Within four years he was reigning as Napoleon III at the head of the Second Empire.

The reverse in Paris blighted the hopes of the champions of freedom everywhere. Disunion among the progressives and nationalists crippled their movement, and gave reaction its opportunity. 1848, so rich in promise, so bitter in disenchantment, had turned out to be a crazy year. The picture was different only in Switzerland, the one country in which the progressives had achieved an enduring triumph. Events there had not waited on Paris; the decisive steps had been taken before revolution swept the other countries; and 1848 was a time of achievement and reconstruction. In Switzerland, it was a creative year.

This outcome owed much to the spirit of moderation which General Dufour and the Diet showed after their triumph over the Sonderbund. Their sense of patriotism and statesmanship made the victors realise that it was more important to establish a fair and orderly system of government than to exact vengeance, which would only have driven a desperate minority to renewed defiance and self-defence. The desirable goal was not a unitary state, although some Radicals were flirting with the idea. A spirit of conciliation was needed to prevent the divisions in the nation from becoming permanent; and it was to the credit of the Swiss people that they paid heed to responsible leaders who advocated such a policy of moderation and compromise. The Bernese Radical, Ulrich Ochsenbein; the progressive Catholic Joseph Munzinger of Solothurn; Johann Konrad Kern from Thurgau; Henri Druey of Vaud; and above all Jonas Furrer of Zürich —these were the men who put their stamp on the work of the committee which rapidly produced a new federal constitution, so ensuring that the year 1848 did not mark a tumultuous interlude in Swiss history but the rational climax to a long process of constitutional advance which was rooted in the traditions and political thinking of the people.

9

The Federal State

I THE 1848 CONSTITUTION

ONE OF the most striking features of the constitution making of 1848 is the speed with which it was carried out. The constitutional revision committee first met in the middle of February, and included representatives of the defeated Sonderbund cantons as well as the victorious majority. Within two months it had produced a draft document for study by the cantons and the Diet. Five months after that the new constitution was overwhelmingly approved.

The central problem was to create a federal system which would promote stability and unity, yet reflect the traditional importance of the cantons. The small cantons—especially the oldest members of the Confederation who were so proud of their ancient rights—wanted a legislature like the Diet in which all cantons were equally represented. But the big cantons like Zürich and Berne pressed for a single chamber elected on the basis of population. To strike a balance between them, the revision committee proposed a bicameral system such as had proved so successful in the United States.

By the end of June, a majority in the Diet had expressed support for the bicameral arrangement and for the proposals as a whole subject to certain amendments. It was now up to the people of the cantons to make their final views known. Early in September it was announced that the new constitution had been approved by fifteen and a half cantons with a population of 1,897,887 and rejected by six and a half cantons representing 292,371 people. The opponents were the Valais, the Ticino, Zug, Unterwalden, Uri, Schwyz and Appenzell-Inner Rhodes—but the first four declared that they would accept a majority decision. On 12 September 1848, the Diet adopted the new constitution as the basic law of the Swiss Confederation.

Jonas Furrer, one of the key figures on the revision committee, had declared in his comment on the original draft: "If the Swiss people accept this federal constitution they may truly claim that it is the first for 50 years which shows no foreign influence; and they can proudly aver that we are the only nation in Europe which in these disjointed times has accomplished the difficult task of political transformation in a peaceful, orderly and constitutional fashion." The transformation had brought into being a system of government which was a sensible and workable compromise between the conflicting tendencies of centralism and a loose confederation of states. It was a synthesis of the experience inherited both from the Napoleonic era and earlier days. The sovereign rights of the cantons were not abolished, but divided between them and the federal state. Because the institutions introduced in 1848 condition the whole of Swiss political life in modern times, it is necessary to describe them in some detail.*

The Federal Parliament

Since the adoption of the 1848 constitution, Switzerland has possessed a Federal Assembly consisting of two chambers with generally equal powers and duties—the Council of States, which represents the cantons, and the National Council, which is representative of the people as a whole.

The Council of States replaced the old Diet; but although it thus became the natural watch-dog of cantonal interests, its members were no longer bound by instructions from the canton governments. From the start, the Council of States has had 44 members, two from each canton irrespective of size and one each from the half-cantons.†

The National Council is a larger body, chosen on a population basis at general elections, held nowadays every four years. Originally, there was one member to every 20,000 inhabitants. But because of the growth of population, the ratio was progressively changed to one member for every 24,000; and in 1962 a fixed number of 200 members was established in the interests of working efficiency.

* In this chapter, the constitutional details have been brought up to date where appropriate; for further information on modern Swiss political life, see final chapter of the book.

† The half-cantons are: Obwalden and Nidwalden, the two parts of Unterwalden since early times; Appenzell Inner and Outer Rhodes, divided in 1597; and Basle-Town and Basle-Country, divided in 1833.

The Federal Assembly meets in Berne, the capital of the Confederation. Legislation requires the approval of a majority in both chambers. They meet in joint session to elect the main authorities of the state : the Federal Council, which is the government of the Confederation; the Federal Tribunal, the highest court in the land; the Federal Chancellor, who is head of the governmental and Assembly secretariat; and the Federal General, the commander-in-chief of the army, who is appointed only in times of emergency.

The Federal Government

The 1848 constitution finally provided the Confederation with a permanent government—the Federal Council. It is a unique institution, quite different from governments in other democratic countries, and has stood the test of time well. The Council is made up of seven members, always men with a wealth of experience in public life. The Federal Assembly elects them individually for a fixed term of four years. But the striking fact is that they are nearly always re-elected for as long as they wish to serve, and in some cases Federal Councillors have remained in office for over 25 years. There has never been a ministerial crisis involving multiple resignations, and this has made for a stability and continuity unknown in other countries.

The membership of the Federal Council is drawn from various parts of Switzerland to reflect the country's cantonal and linguistic components; and although in the 19th century it was dominated by the Radicals, the driving force in the reform movement, it is now representative as far as its small size permits of all the big political parties—Radicals, Conservatives, Social Democrats and Farmers. Throughout its existence it has practised a collegiate system of government, with important decisions being taken by all seven members as a body carrying collective responsibility.

Each Federal Councillor is the head of one of the seven administrative departments into which Swiss federal government is organised. The President of the Confederation is chosen by the Assembly from among the members of the Federal Council, but he is allowed only a year in office at any one time and is considered simply "the first among equals." Like the constitution as a whole, this reflects the traditional distaste for any form of one-man rule. It is efficient, self-effacing administrative ability that is expected from the Federal Council, not oratory or the skills of party politics. Although the councillors appear before the Assembly, they are not members of it and are not "responsible" to it in the sense that they need not resign if their policies are rejected. Constitutionally, members of both the Assembly and of the Federal Council can introduce bills, but in practice most legislation is initiated by the Council.

The pattern of the new system was drawn from cantonal experience, and the foundation of its success was laid by the very first Federal Council. Its seven members were Jonas Furrer from Winterthur; Ulrich Ochsenbein from Thun; Joseph Munzinger from Olten; Henri Druey from Vaud; Stefano Franscini from the Ticino; Friedrich Frey-Hérosé from Aarau; and Wilhelm Näff from St. Gallen. All of them made an important contribution to their country's development in this creative period of its history. Furrer, who had done so much to help evolve the new constitutional system, was the first Federal President. The son of a locksmith, he had built up a flourishing legal practice in his native canton, but a sense of duty inspired him to give up his lucrative profession to serve Switzerland, although the state paid its chief executive so badly that he depended on a subsidy from his home town. Furrer was not the man to complain about that; under the new democratic system many Federal Councillors came from humble families, and Stefano Franscini's home in Bodio bore the inscription : "He was born, lived and died poor."

The Role of the Cantons

Article three of the Swiss constitution says : "The cantons are sovereign as far as their sovereignty is not limited by the federal constitution, and as such they exercise all rights which are not delegated to the federal power." From 1848, these delegated rights were extensive. Firstly, the federal state took over the conduct of foreign affairs. The cantons, like the federal government, were forbidden to enter into mercenary service agreements with foreign powers; and in a reminder of the Sonderbund, the cantons were not allowed to conclude separate alliances of a political nature among themselves. The federal state was given more control over the army, although without achieving complete unification, and no canton could normally maintain a standing force of more than 300 men without federal permission. With the acceptance of compulsory military service, an ancient tradition in the cantons, the central government could now aim at ensuring that its policy of neutrality would be defended by a uniformly trained national army. This military organisation has since developed in such a way that modern Switzerland can put 400,000 troops in the field at short notice. They are members of an efficient fully-equipped militia, not a standing army, and Switzerland keeps only a small nucleus of professional soldiers. The system is that all men are liable for military service. Between the ages of 20 and 50 (55 in the case of officers) all those found fit for service undergo first a spell of basic training and then periodic refresher courses.

In other matters, too, the new era produced greater unity. At last there was a central authority with the power and funds to create a national economic framework without which Switzerland could never have become a leading industrialised state and a centre of the financial world. Tariffs and customs, hitherto matters for the individual cantons, came under federal control in 1848. The countless internal tariffs were finally abolished and revenue from the frontier customs flowed into the federal treasury, though direct taxation was reserved to the cantons. The postal service became a federal matter, followed by the telegraph and in later years broadcasting. Weights and measures were also unified; and the state put an end to the bewildering profusion of more than 300 different coins by the introduction in 1850 of a single currency, the Swiss franc.

While the cantons sacrificed much of their authority to the common good, they have retained their governing councils, though changes in their constitutions are subject to the approval of the federal government. To this day the cantons have also maintained primary responsibility for law enforcement and for the provision of education on the understanding that freedom of conscience and religion are guaranteed. Moreover, the institution of Swiss federal citizenship is based on the cantons and the smaller units, the communes. To be a Swiss citizen a person must have cantonal citizenship, which in turn depends on being a citizen of one of the 3,095 communes that are the foundation of Swiss society. From the start, the federal government has depended heavily on the cantons to see that the whole system works, and they in turn have gained from the unity established in 1848. It was a partnership created by the cantons themselves, and that has been its strength.

Liberty and the Law

One of the priorities of the 1848 constitution was to protect the people's rights and liberties, and this even came before the promotion of material well-being. The democratic principle of equality before the law was guaranteed in the constitution, which ruled out any privilege by virtue of place, birth, person or family. Freedom of association was guaranteed, and so was freedom of the press. From now on, too, Catholics and Protestants were assured equal rights of worship and religious observance, though the Jesuits were finally banned. Freedom of settlement led to people of the two Churches mixing more and getting to know each other better.

Under the Swiss legal system, the lower levels of jurisdiction are left in the hands of the cantonal courts and it is their job to enforce federal and cantonal law. But the Federal Tribunal, whose powers have grown through the years, is the supreme court in civil law cases, the ultimate court of appeal in criminal matters and is entrusted with the protection of the citizens' constitutional rights. The Tribunal can declare a cantonal law invalid and is empowered to hear appeals from actions of cantonal executives; but it has no power to enquire into the constitutionality of federal laws, unlike the Federal Supreme Court in the United States. Its judges are elected by the Federal Assembly for six-year terms but are usually re-elected to serve until they are 70.

II THE GROWTH OF DEMOCRACY

The year of revolutions in Europe had provided Switzerland with a federal constitution which was a product of the most vigorous liberal ideas and had skilfully fused together the strands of unity broken in the Sonderbund war. Switzerland had become a representative democracy more attuned to the aspirations of its people. Nevertheless, the demand for a greater degree of direct participation in the running of the country was to dominate political debate in the years ahead. External affairs were also to have a significant influence, for republican Switzerland could not isolate itself from events in the surrounding monarchies, particularly the emergence of a powerful nationalism in Germany, which brought about the defeat of France in the war of 1870. But before this stage of history was reached, Switzerland had to try to resolve the outstanding political tensions within its own society.

Sound political judgement had made the Swiss leaders realise that flexibility was needed in the 1848 constitution. They avoided the cardinal mistake of the Federal Pact of 1815, which rigidly excluded any provision for lawful amendment and in the end made the people resort to arms to establish a new society. The 1848 constitution specifically stated that it could be revised at any time and the people were given the last say in the matter. Two instruments of this direct democracy in Switzerland are the *compulsory constitutional referendum* and the *popular constitutional initiative*.

Any change in the federal constitution must to this day be approved in a national referendum. A majority of all voters and a majority of the cantons is needed. In most cases it is the Federal Council or the Federal Assembly which propose such changes. But the people themselves can make a request for the constitution to be revised in part or as a whole. This is their right of popular initiative. It can be exercised by way of a petition signed by at least 50,000 registered voters, who can either submit their own detailed draft of an amendment or ask the legislature to work it out. In the end, the proposal is put to the vote in the country.

Though the popular initiative has been frequently used, few constitutional changes so demanded have in fact won popular acceptance. In general, the people seem to be content to let government and parliament set the process of change in motion. Since 1848 well over 50 of the legislature's amendments have been accepted. The very first referendum under the federal constitution, in 1866, came at the suggestion of the government. It succeeded in amending the constitution to grant Jews in Switzerland freedom of settlement and freedom to practice a trade. This recommendation had been put forward after France had said it would conclude a trade treaty only if all French residents in Switzerland were guaranteed these rights, irrespective of their religion.

The third instrument of direct democracy in Switzerland is the *legislative referendum*. As a general rule, laws passed by the Federal Assembly and major international treaties are open to popular challenge. The people can demand a referendum on them by submitting a petition signed by at least 30,000 voters or eight cantons, but this must be done within 90 days of the publication of the law. In a referendum, the law is considered rejected if a majority of the people vote against it: no majority of the cantons is needed as when a change in the constitution is involved.

The legislative referendum was not introduced at federal level until the constitution was revised in 1874, although it had been used in some of the cantons well before that. It was the outcome of the people's demand to be even more closely involved in the running of the country. For although representative democracy had brought considerable progress, it tended to be dominated by the new ruling class of Liberal-Radical leaders. The system run by these federal magnates, as they were known, was repugnant to a generation which was politically much more mature than its predecessors thanks to improved education and a free press. With policy decisions being made by prosperous industrialists and city bosses, people felt their vote meant little and only about one in five went to the polls. The federal magnates seemed to be guided by the slogan "everything for the people, nothing through the people." It was suspiciously reminiscent of the period of aristocratic rule; and this state of affairs led in the 1860's to the rise in many cantons of a new Democratic movement.

Ordinary people from all walks of life began to organise themselves. Peasants, artisans, the working class, all pinned their hopes on having a direct say in legislation. The peasants wanted to bring about a reduction in irksome taxes; the increasingly powerful artisans looked for cheaper credit from newly-founded cantonal banks; and the workers pressed for shorter hours and better conditions than those provided under existing laws, which regulated only the conditions of children's employment and allowed even them to work up to 13 hours a day. These groups felt that swift improvement could only be achieved when the people were not simply voters but also lawmakers.

In this struggle for more direct democracy the lead was taken by Basle-Country, which in 1863 became the first to introduce the legislative referendum into a cantonal constitution. Not only that: it also provided for the *popular legislative initiative*, which enabled the people to submit their own proposals for new laws. In addition, they won the right to elect not only the canton's legislature but also members of its executive and judiciary. Through the ballot, the people in Basle-Country were now effectively law-makers, as for many centuries the full citizens of the *Landsgemeinde* cantons had been through their public vote in the ring. The original idea of the Swiss communities had found its modern democratic expression.

Though the pioneering innovations of the Basle constitution were important, it was the change of attitude in Zürich which proved of crucial significance for the ultimate triumph of the Democrats' ideas in the rest of Switzerland. In Zürich, the system of the federal magnates was personified in the remarkable Alfred Escher. The son of a wealthy family, Escher studied law in Germany and was already burgomaster of Zürich and its dominant personality when he was only 29. The following year he was president of the National Council, a post he held on three further occasions. The rapid development of Zürich's economy and transport system should be credited to Escher's vision; and the critics who assailed him bitterly as the "banklord" and "railway king" did him less than justice. Even when Escher was no longer a member of the Zürich government, he was untiringly active in public affairs. Important people in the world of finance, letters and fashion would gather at his country residence, Belvoir, and Escher held all the threads of the upper class network in his hands. But this involvement estranged him increasingly from the man in the street. Moreover, the combination of politics with business had its risks and caused resentment.

The reaction against Escher was seen in the winter of 1867. Although the weather was bad for political meetings, his opponents obtained not just the 10,000 signatures necessary under Zürich law for demanding a revision of the constitution, but nearly three times as many. Two years later, a popular ballot produced a 90 per cent poll, demonstrating the public interest in direct democracy. More than three-fifths of the electors voted for a new constitutional law which widened the people's power. It introduced the legislative referendum and popular legislative initiative, created a cantonal bank and abolished the death penalty and the imprisonment of debtors. From now on, Article One of the Zürich constitution declared: "The power of the state rests on the people as a whole. It is exercised directly through the citizens, and only indirectly through the authorities and officials." The role of the cantonal council had changed: it was

no longer authoritarian as in the past but had become essentially a
consultative institution.

The poet Gottfried Keller, who was the cantonal secretary, greeted
the change as a bloodless revolution, just as he had welcomed the
federal constitution of 1848. Under the new system in Zürich an
entirely different kind of politician emerged, and the gloomy proph-
ecies of the dethroned magnates and bureaucrats were not fulfilled. Encouraged by Zürich's example, other cantons followed suit:
Thurgau, Aargau, Solothurn, Lucerne and Berne all modified their
constitutions on the same lines. This meant victory for direct democracy in most of the cantons which earlier in the century had emu-
lated Zürich in the drive for regeneration. The question now was
whether Switzerland as a whole ought to revise the federal constitution to incorporate the ideas which the cantons were trying out on
a more limited scale.

III   THE CONSTITUTIONAL REVISION

Events in Europe cast their shadow on Switzerland as the people
debated whether to support a total revision of the federal constitution.
The main external force to be reckoned with was German nationalism
after France had been defeated in the war of 1870. The mighty new
German fatherland was a challenge to all its neighbours. In the
Franco-Prussian war, the Swiss Federal Council stuck to the policy
of neutrality; but with the new dangers on the borders it was abund-
antly clear that a more powerful army was needed to safeguard
Switzerland's security and neutrality, and that in other ways, too, the
Confederation must be knit more closely together.

Once again in Swiss history, religious pressures also had a bearing
on events, and led to demands for sharper constitutional provisions
against militant Catholicism. In 1870, tense relations arose between
the Confederation and the Catholic Church over the Vatican declaration of Papal infallibility in matters of faith and morals. The Radicals, who stood for the supremacy of secular power, found this dogma
incompatible with their beliefs, and Protestants as a whole regarded
it as arrogance. Opposition also sprang up from the Old Catholics,
who considered that the dogma conflicted with the traditional faith
of the Church and were supported in their attitude by the state

authorities. The dispute between Church and state was particularly sharp in Geneva. It ultimately led to the abolition of the Papal Nunciate, which had existed for three centuries; and it was not until 1920 that a Papal Nuncio returned to Switzerland.

As the time came for a decision on revising the federal constitution, the Swiss people were therefore faced with powerful internal and external pressures. The two main issues were: Should the people have a greater say in legislation? And should the powers of the federal state be strengthened for the sake of the country's security and stability even at the expense of some individual liberty? Those who looked first to cantonal interests were resolutely opposed to greater centralism. The political opposition was led by the Catholic Conservatives, who stoutly championed the cantons' autonomy in the face of the overwhelming power of the Radicals in the National Council and the Federal Council. The Conservatives regarded the Radical proposals for strengthening the federal state as dangerous and authoritarian—and it did not lessen their alarm to see that centralism was being supported by the Swiss Social Democrats, whose party was founded in 1870.

As for the centralists, they campaigned for the total revision of the constitution under the slogan "One law, one army." Most people saw the sense of unifying the military system, with the co-ordinated training that was necessary to produce an effective force. But there was opposition to the proposal to centralise civil and criminal law and legal procedure, especially from the French-speaking areas and the old cantons of central Switzerland. When it came to the point, many people also had doubts about the idea of introducing the legislative referendum and the popular legislative initiative at federal level.

The decision went against the proposals as a whole when they were put to the vote in 1872. Thirteen cantons rejected them and only nine approved. The popular vote, however, was much more closely balanced: 261,000 against, 256,000 in favour. This outcome encouraged the advocates of constitutional revision, led by the respected Federal Councillor from Aargau, Emil Welti. They were now prepared to make compromises to get the proposals accepted. To win over the French-speaking Swiss, many of whom were unwilling to give up their cantonal autonomy and were apprehensive of too much Germanisation, some of the centralising features in the proposals were

watered down. In addition, Lausanne, capital of Vaud, was nominated as the permanent seat of the Federal Tribunal. The cantons were
also promised a bigger role than originally envisaged in the administration of the army and the law.

The legislative referendum was included in the draft proposals.
But the legislative initiative, for which many had fought in the hope
of giving the people a greater say in law-making, was not accepted
and has never become part of the federal constitution. On religion,
the proposals took a strong stand against militant Catholicism. Education at elementary level in the cantons was to be compulsory, free
and inter-denominational. Labour law was to be extended to give
the state overall supervision of factory work.

On 19 April 1874, the revised federal constitution with the above
provisions was adopted by $14\frac{1}{2}$ to $7\frac{1}{2}$ cantons; 340,000 popular votes
were cast for it, 198,00 against. With later modifications, it has since
remained the foundation of the Swiss Confederation. In strengthening
the state, there is no doubt the Swiss people were prompted by the
knowledge that their immediate neighbours, Italy as well as Germany,
had become powerful nation-states and that Switzerland could hold
its own only in unity. When in the 20th century moderate regimes
in those two countries were swept away by the torrent of whipped-up
nationalism under the dictatorships of Hitler and Mussolini, there
were renewed stirrings in Switzerland for another total revision of the
constitution. But the popular vote in the autumn of 1935 showed
that the people as a whole did not feel the uncertain conditions of
those days made such a change advisable, although they have constantly kept the constitution under review, all the time endeavouring
to improve it by amendments.

One major change came in 1919 with the use of a system of proportional representation for elections to the National Council. By
ensuring that parties were represented according to their relative
strength, the system meant the end of Radical dominance in the
federal government and enabled minority groups to make their voices
better heard in the affairs of the nation. As with many other reforms
in Switzerland, proportional representation began at cantonal level.
It was introduced in the Ticino in 1892 after a struggle for power
between the Radicals and Conservatives had led to violence and
federal intervention. Later the system was adopted in other cantons.

The years after the first world war saw a demonstration of the way the Swiss voter can bring his views to bear directly on foreign policy as well as on internal affairs. Switzerland was the only country to hold a referendum on joining the League of Nations, and the vote went narrowly in favour after keen debate among the people. One big advantage of the referendum in Switzerland is that it encourages this sort of open debate and acts as a political safety valve, ensuring that criticism is not driven underground. The Swiss, of course, often curse their government, but at least they have the democratic right to change their legislators and challenge the laws they make. At one time, pessimists used to argue that to grant wider rights to the people meant a threat of permanent revolution. It is quite true that it is only too easy to collect 30,000 signatures, for example, to demand a legislative referendum to challenge a law; this number once represented 4 per cent of the electorate, while today it amounts to less than 2 per cent. In practice, however, the people have often used their votes to put the brake on proposed legislation—certainly more often than impatient reformers might have liked. But such delay has frequently turned out to be of benefit to the country by giving more time for thorough revision of legislative proposals after all the issues have been thrashed out.

In one important sphere, the enfranchisement of women in federal affairs, a great deal remains to be done. In this matter Switzerland is out of line with most modern democracies. While male citizens on reaching the age of 20 are entitled to vote and stand as candidates, women do not have these rights at federal level. It has been argued that because the civic powers and duties which suffrage involves are more extensive in Switzerland than elsewhere, male voters have been reluctant to grant women equal political status. Unfortunately, the example set by the men is by no means always inspiring. Their voting record leaves much to be desired, with the average poll over the years sometimes dropping to around 50 per cent, giving some foreigners the false impression that many Swiss feel they have too much democracy and are fed up with it. In any event, as late as 1959 the men rejected by a two-thirds majority a constitutional proposal by the federal legislature to give women equal political right.* So there was no change at the federal level. But in the last ten years reform has been approved by the electorate in the cantons of Vaud, Neuchâtel,

Geneva, Basle, Ticino, and Fribourg. Women now have the vote at communal and cantonal level and are eligible for public office. Progress has also been made elsewhere : Grisons, Berne and Zürich have allowed women a say in communal policies; and in many other cantons, too, they play their part in educational and church affairs and the judicial service.

*Swiss women were granted the federal vote for the first time in the country's history in a national referendum on 7 February 1971. Voting was 621,403 in favour and 323,596 against, in a 57 per cent poll.

10

Economic Progress

I INDUSTRIALISATION AND SOCIAL CHANGE

A S THE 22 cantons of 19th century Switzerland sought to strengthen their unity without sacrificing their diversity, there was a close interaction between the dynamic forces of politics and the limiting factors of geography, both moulding the country's future in the now vitally important sphere of economic development. Constitutional reform promoted industrial and commercial advance by bringing down barriers between the cantons and encouraging unity of purpose among them, whether they owed their distinctive character to the traditions of the ancient rural communities or to the progressive enterprise of the towns. For all of them, internationally-recognised neutrality created the conditions under which a small nation with more than 1,000 miles of frontiers could live amidst the rival giants of Europe and yet be spared the economic destruction of modern war. But the specific economic course that Switzerland took, different in so many ways from that of its big neighbours, was dictated by quite basic factors. Those 1,000 miles of frontiers enclosed a little country with a population of less than two-and-a-half millions in 1850; a country at a cross-roads of Europe, yet far from the world-wide routes of the ocean traders; above all, a country crisscrossed by mountains and lakes, with only three-quarters of its land productive, and with virtually no coal or other mineral deposits.

The small landlocked Confederation was certainly under no temptation to emulate other western countries in seeking overseas colonial possessions as sources of wealth or potential markets. Yet with no raw materials to speak of, it had to trade abroad to get them; and with no ready-made markets, it had to use every resource to find outlets for its goods. The Swiss weavers, spinners and watchmakers had to adapt themselves to the changing conditions of factory production and world-wide commerce.

To compensate for the lack of natural resources, Switzerland had to make the most of its important assets: water power and human enterprise. Water power from the Alpine glaciers and the rivers of the lowlands was harnessed to drive the wheels of the new factories and eventually to provide electricity in abundance for the country's modern industries and its railways, which are now fully electrified. The fact that industry followed water power accounts for the great contrast with those nations which have built their fortunes on coal. Swiss factories were dispersed through the country, avoiding the harmful concentrations which blackened the landscape in other European regions and blighted the lives of their working people. In this sense, the lack of coal was an advantage for Switzerland: the dispersal of industry meant that factory life was more tolerable and the people kept contact with the land. The gulf between town and country, so marked in some industrial societies, went far less deep.

From the outset of the modern industrial age, Swiss businessmen and craftsmen surmounted their country's handicaps with the same adaptability as the Protestant refugees had shown in the 16th and 17th centuries when they made an enduring contribution to the industries and culture of the reformed cities of the Confederation. A major factor in harnessing Switzerland's human resources has been the country's system of training and education, rapidly developed in the 19th century. Trade schools were opened to give thorough instruction in specialised skills, and the most up-to-date facilities were made available at the Federal Institute of Technology in Zürich, which since its foundation has built up an international reputation. The Institute was opened by the Confederation under the educational provisions of the 1848 constitution, but the expansion of universities was left in the hands of the cantons. The seven cantonal universities, which demonstrate the varied cultural life of the Confederation, cater in our day for about 30,000 students, and nearly a quarter of the total student population in Switzerland is made up of young people from abroad.

The emphasis on training in the 19th century ensured that Swiss products retained the hallmark of quality on which they have greatly depended in competing with the mass-production industries of bigger countries. Machines had been brought into the lives of the workers, but meticulous attention continued to be given to craftsmanship. In this way the Swiss maintained the high repute established over centuries by such industries as the watch-making of Geneva and the Jura, the silks and textiles of Zürich and Basle, the linens, cottons and embroidery of St. Gallen.

In the long history of Swiss industries, textile manufacture takes pride of place, though it has suffered many setbacks over the years. Modern development began when the first spinning machine was installed in 1799 in the monastery of St. Gallen, which had been abandoned by the monks. The industry prospered to such a degree that there were two million spindles in the country by 1872. The pace-setter was Heinrich Kunz of Zürich, the king of the spinners. Kunz came to employ more than 2,000 workers in 11 mills despite the fierce opposition his factory system encountered from cottage workers who feared the introduction of machines would leave them unemployed. In fact mechanisation brought prosperity: by 1864 cotton printing in Glarus, for instance, offered work to more than 6,000 people engaged in producing colourful cloth that was tremendously popular abroad. But towards the end of the 19th century sales fell away sharply and factories had to be converted to other uses. The decline was, however, delayed in embroidery, which at the beginning of the 20th century enjoyed great prosperity in St. Gallen and Appenzell, where the work was still carried out to a large extent by cottage workers. They finally fell on hard times when export markets suddenly dried up after 1920.

The end of the golden age forced employers and workers to switch to goods which were less crisis-prone than textiles and not so much affected by changes of fashion. Consequently, although textile manufacture still has its significant place in the Swiss economy, it has long been overtaken in importance by an industry which sprang from it, mechanical engineering. In the early days, Swiss textile producers imported their machines from Britain and adapted them for their own needs. In time, however, Switzerland was not only making its own machines but also exporting them, so laying the foundations for a highly-diversified modern engineering industry which is of supreme importance to the economy. The turn of the century also saw lively development in another sector: the chemical and pharmaceutical industry, which had its beginnings in the production of dyestuffs for Switzerland's fabrics and is now a flourishing branch of the country's export trade.

Of Switzerland's oldest industries, the one with the most consistent performance and unrivalled reputation is watch and clock-making. At one time it was closely linked with the art of the goldsmith, of which the Church was a great patron. After the Reformation, however, the number of Church commissions declined, and so artists and craftsmen began to apply their skill to producing clocks and watches for the market. This development brought great commercial benefits to the Jura region, which had followed Geneva in the watch-making craft, and this regional enterprise has ever since been one of Switzerland's major money-earners.

As Switzerland developed into a modern industrial nation, depending on the import of raw materials and the export of finished products, its agriculture gradually declined. With the import of cheap corn, the farmers cut down on their grain crops; the emphasis switched to dairy farming and stock-breeding, allied to a food industry based largely on milk products, and since the middle of the 19th century the number of cattle has doubled. Swiss farmers introduced mechanisation reluctantly, and small to medium-scale farming remained the rule. State subsidies were brought in to assist the farmers, and they did what they could to help themselves, for example by forming agricultural associations to look after their supplies and marketing. In 1897, these groups merged to set up the Swiss Farmers' Association.

Despite the decline in its numbers the farming community remained an important and influential part of the nation, while with the dispersal of factories industrial Switzerland, too, kept roots in the countryside. Nevertheless, 19th century developments inevitably involved a big movement of population to the towns. In 1850 there were only eight towns with more than 10,000 inhabitants, and their total population numbered only 154,000. By the end of the century Zürich alone had a population of more than 150,000; and at the end of the 1960's it had increased to nearly 440,000, although Switzerland has never become a country of huge cities.

Industrialisation and the social changes that went with it brought the Swiss closer together. With the coming of the machine age, people moved their homes and jobs regardless of religious and political barriers, which had hitherto divided the Confederation; and this transformation was vitally influenced by the liberties enshrined in the 1848 constitution—the freedoms of expression, conscience, trade and settlement. Protestant churches sprang up in the old Catholic cantons of central Switzerland; and in Zürich, the city of Zwingli, there are today more Catholics than in any other Swiss town. Rural areas found themselves with factories, and towns recruited workers who retained their links with the countryside. As a result of this process, it is no longer possible to speak simply of town and rural cantons and Catholic and Protestant ones as in the past. Nobody was compelled to change his political or religious allegiance on moving from one canton to another, although when families decided to settle in different linguistic areas the children at least found it quite natural to adopt the new language. But language of itself was no barrier, and linguistic issues rarely poisoned politics as happened in some other countries.

II THE GROWING ROLE OF THE STATE

In promoting greater unity, a major role was played by mechanised transport and communications, which made travel and the exchange of goods easier and helped to spread knowledge and information more quickly. The beginning of the railway age in Switzerland coincided almost exactly with the new constitution. In 1845, the first steam train rolled on to Swiss soil, arriving in Basle from Strasbourg, and two years later the first domestic line was opened from Zürich to Baden. A railway boom followed, and it was over the railways that the first major debate on state intervention developed.

The state was given control of the railways only in 1898 at the end of a prolonged and hotly argued dispute between the protagonists of private railways and those who advocated a state-controlled system. In the early days of the debate, the Zürich financier Alfred Escher, who gave his powerful leadership to the private enterprise campaign, succeeded in outsmarting his great opponent, Federal Councillor Jakob Stämpfli of Berne, a man of the people and the most determined spokesman for a state railway. Only when more and more people realised that the railway companies were feathering the share-

holders' nests instead of serving the country at large did the slogan
"The Swiss railways for the Swiss people!" begin to make an impact.

In 1852 a large majority in the Federal Assembly voted for private
railways, with almost no central control. Ten years later Stämpfli,
then President of the Confederation, once more pleaded for nationali-
sation, but again unsuccessfully. It was not until 1898 that more than
two-thirds of the voters supported state control when the issue was put
to a popular ballot. In this way, out of four separate companies the
basic network of the Swiss Federal Railways was created. Later it was
augmented by the important trans-Alpine Gotthard line, which had
been opened in 1882. The establishment of this line was due to the
business drive of Alfred Escher and the engineering brilliance of
Louis Favre of Geneva, helped by emergency support from the Confederation which shouldered responsibility for additional finance when
it was found that construction costs were exceeding the estimates.

Railway management had confronted the Swiss with a debate on
state intervention in industry within very few years of the founding
of the modern Confederation. The state's responsibility towards the
working people was another urgent issue resulting from increased
industrialisation. Today it is difficult to imagine under what pitiable
conditions women and children were employed 100 years ago. In
1866, the poet Gottfried Keller castigated the mill owners who made
children work 13 hours a day in their factories. He believed a humanitarian state must discharge its social obligations. After all, the
constitution proclaimed concern for promoting the general well-being;
and if this was not to remain an empty phrase, a state reorganised
on liberal and democratic lines had to take action and introduce
social welfare legislation.

As in other matters, such law-making followed the Swiss pattern
of gradually adopting on a federal level the experience initially gained
by the cantons. The first move was to incorporate the guiding principles in the federal constitution. But laws to implement them did
not always follow so swiftly as the Factory Act of 1877, which came
only three years after the constitutional revision. The 1877 Act,
which reduced the working day to 11 hours and prohibited child
labour, was the foundation on which Switzerland has step by step
built a modern code of labour law. Many anxious years were to
pass, however, before the next major social reform advanced from

principle to practice. In 1890, a constitutional clause was adopted envisaging state aid for workers who were sick or injured, but it was not until 1911 that the Sickness and Accident Insurance Act became law. It made provision for adequate compensation in case of diminished working capacity, and granted benefits of up to 70 per cent of annual earnings in case of total disability and 60 per cent to the dependants of a worker killed in an accident.

For the people of Switzerland their country's successful adaptation to the industrial age meant one supremely important thing: there was work available for all. In times past it had been a struggle to feed and clothe the population, and mercenary service had been a way out for young men seeking a livelihood. Now the situation had changed: there were plenty of opportunities at home. It is true that in the early period of the federal state about 15,000 people a year sought their fortune in other countries; but emigration came to play a far less significant role and one outstanding feature since the 19th century has been the mass of people travelling the other way—foreign workers and, of course, the tourists.

Travel in the Alps had already become popular in the 18th century, at least among a minority influenced by the work of writers, artists and naturalists who had revealed the romantic beauty and scientific interest of the great mountains. A steady flow of foreigners visited Switzerland, and the number increased throughout the 19th century with the rise of modern means of transport and the growing appeal of mountaineering. First the British and then people of other nations came to test their skill and endurance against the Alpine summits, and the pioneers paved the way for the wider popularity of mountain-climbing, skiing and other winter sports. The beauty of the landscape, the challenge of the peaks, and the health of the Alpine air became economic assets. More and more hotels were opened to cater for the expanding tourist trade, offering thousands of people employment. Tourism, the creation of the railway age, has since become one of the mainsprings of Switzerland's economy and has made a vital contribution to its financial strength.

11

The Years of Trial

I SWISS FOREIGN POLICY 1848–1914

FROM 1848 onwards Switzerland's relations with other countries
were guided by two principles: a unified foreign policy under
the control of the federal authorities, not the cantons, and
strict neutrality based on Swiss traditions and international agreement. The wisdom of this course in safeguarding the integrity and
unity of the Confederation was clearly shown during the series of
nationalist upheavals and wars which affected all its great neighbours and drastically changed the map of Europe. But at first the
more extreme Radicals did not find it an easy policy to accept. In
the revolutionary atmosphere of the mid-19th century, they were
anxious that Switzerland should demonstrate where its sympathies
lay. Solidarity with those struggling for freedom inspired them; non-
intervention did not. Their enthusiasm for the cause of liberty
might have rushed Switzerland into a foreign adventure even before
its new constitution was complete. In the spring of 1848, the king of
neighbouring Piedmont sought a Swiss alliance against the Austrian
empire as part of the design to liberate Italy. The idea of sending
30,000 troops to help the Italians against the Habsburgs found support among some Radicals, but a majority in the Diet firmly rejected
an alliance which would have meant a complete reversal of the
policy of neutrality.

The collapse of the freedom movements in various parts of Europe
in 1848 imposed a great strain on Switzerland's neutrality and on
its relations with the continental powers, particularly because of the
widespread Swiss sympathy for the progressives and the reception
given to the large numbers of refugees who poured into the country.
Among the 15,000 who sought asylum from political persecution by
the royalist rulers were artists and scholars who contributed greatly

to Swiss intellectual life—men like Richard Wagner, the poet Ferdinand Freiligrath, and the architect Gottfried Semper, who built the renowned Federal Institute of Technology in Zürich. Switzerland had often been a haven for refugees in the past and was to be again in the future—in the 1860s, for example, when many Poles fled there after their abortive rising against the Russians. The Swiss greeted such refugees as champions of freedom. The strength of public feeling for the principles of liberty and humanity was also made clear in the messages of support for the north in the American civil war and the way the Swiss went into mourning when news reached them of the murder of Abraham Lincoln.

Although there was no doubting the depth of Swiss feeling in these struggles of the 19th century, the Federal Council was anxious that refugees should not abuse their position by plotting against foreign rulers; and those that did so found themselves losing sympathy. To the continental powers, however, the mere existence of this refuge for republicans in the heart of Europe was a constant source of irritation, and at one time there was talk among them of intervention. In the event, such talk came to nothing. But a series of incidents did arise in which Switzerland's security was threatened in turn by Austria, Prussia and France.

The first such incident took place in the south, where in the 1850s the Italian-speaking Swiss of the Ticino were roused to enthusiasm by the campaign in northern Italy against the Austrians and all their trappings of power. In 1852, the canton of Ticino removed two seminaries from the administration of Italian bishops and expelled 22 Capuchin monks for subversive activities. Austria reacted angrily with the expulsion of 6,000 Ticinese from Lombardy. It also took the drastic course of imposing a food blockade on the Ticino. This blow at Switzerland's vulnerable supply routes produced an ugly situation, and the blockade was only lifted when agreement was reached to pay compensation to the expelled Capuchins.

To the north, tension had already arisen in 1849, when the Swiss were involved in an incident after a rising in the German state of Baden. A small German force which had intruded was escorted back to Baden by Swiss units. But this was a minor affair compared to the crisis that developed a few years later in Switzerland's relations with the most powerful of the German states, Prussia. The crisis arose over Prussia's claims in the canton of Neuchâtel, and it nearly brought the Confederation to disaster.

Since 1707, Neuchâtel had been a principality of the King of Prussia and was under his nominal control; but at the Congress of Vienna in 1815 it had also been given equal status with other Swiss cantons. During the Sonderbund war Neuchâtel remained neutral; but as soon as the news of the 1848 revolution in Paris reached the principality, the workers at La Chaux-de-Fonds and Le Locle overthrew the royalists who governed in the name of the King of Prussia and set up a republic. Although the triumphant republicans had broken the bond with Prussia, however, the great powers still in principle recognised King Frederick William's title to the territory. Thus encouraged, the Neuchâtel royalists rebelled in September 1856 and defiantly hoisted the royal flag above the castle. But the romantic interlude was brief. The following day the republicans stormed the castle. The clash claimed few casualties and most of the 700 captured royalists were soon released; but there was insistence on holding the ringleaders until Prussia formally renounced all claim to Neuchâtel. The King of Prussia regarded this as "a slap in the face for all monarchs" and urged the powers to intervene. The German states along with Austria, Russia and France gave him moral support, but were not prepared to risk war in the heart of Europe over a rebellion in Neuchâtel. Napoleon III, in particular, had no wish whatever to see Prussian troops on the south-eastern border of France. His exile at Arenenberg had also taught him that the Swiss would not yield to foreign pressure; and so it turned out when, at the beginning of 1857, Prussia mobilised.

A wave of patriotism swept through Switzerland, and the Federal Council was determined to fight if necessary. Once more the nation closed its ranks around Dufour, who was re-elected General and given 30,000 troops for an advance into southern Germany in case of war. But hostilities were averted, thanks largely to mediation by Napoleon III at the request of the British government, which urged moderation on its friends in Switzerland and brought strong pressure to bear on King Frederick William. A peaceful settlement and an end to the irregular constitutional position of Neuchâtel was finally achieved. The Swiss agreed to release the remaining royalist prisoners, and the Prussian King renounced his sovereign rights over the distant principality, retaining only the title of "Prince of Neuchâtel and Count of Valengin." So Neuchâtel remained a Swiss canton: the dangerous episode had ended in a success for Swiss policy and a demonstration that the country was prepared to defend its territorial integrity.

Though Napoleon III, the former honorary citizen of Thurgau, had appeared as mediator in the Neuchâtel crisis, Switzerland was soon to learn that it could not count on him when French interests were at stake. Trouble arose over a bargain he made with Piedmont at the time of the Italian war of independence of 1859. France had helped the Italians defeat the Austrians, and in recognition of this assistance was to be given Savoy and Nice by the King of Piedmont. But the northern part of Savoy, adjoining Lake Geneva, had been neutralised by treaty since 1815, and the Swiss had been given the right to occupy the area for their own security in the event of war between their neighbours. When Napoleon III ignored this treaty right and annexed the whole of Savoy in 1860 without even informing Switzerland, the uproar started. The Federal President of the time, Jakob Stämpfli, who had stood up to Prussia over Neuchâtel, protested vigorously to France and began to get belligerent, but this time without much popular support. Napoleon III showed greater diplomatic skill. He quickly organised a plebiscite in Savoy, mounting a propaganda campaign and giving an assurance of customs-free trade with Geneva, the natural market of the people in north Savoy. The vote went in favour of union with France. Switzerland's theoretical rights in the neutralised area were finally abolished in 1918, but the free trade zones have remained, with the support of the International Court.

The war of Italian independence led to the emergence in the south of a united Italy, a new factor in the European situation. During the war, the Federal Council took great pains to protect Swiss security and neutrality, and when 650 Austrian troops escaped over the frontier into the Ticino they were immediately interned. At this time, too, Switzerland took steps to emphasise its neutrality by clarifying its attitude over the question of foreign military service. The 1848 constitution had forbidden any new contracts to supply mercenary troops to foreign powers; but under existing agreements there were still 12,000 Swiss mercenaries serving the court of Naples. In 1859, the Confederation prohibited both recruitment of mercenary troops and enlistment in Swiss regiments abroad. Only service in the regular national armies of other countries was allowed. This was not abolished until 1927 after about 10,000 Swiss had fought in the first world war, chiefly on the side of the western powers. Since then the Pope's Swiss Guard, a picturesque force of 133 men, has been the only remnant of the days when Switzerland was a favourite recruiting ground for foreign rulers.

If the events in the south demanded vigilance of the Swiss and a clear restatement of their neutrality, developments in Germany posed a much more serious political and military problem. In 1861, William I came to the throne of Prussia. The following year Bismarck became his chancellor. By the end of the decade they had fought three decisive wars as a preliminary to the establishment of a Prussian-dominated German empire. In the first war, Schleswig-Holstein was torn from Denmark; in the second, Austria was forcibly excluded from a say in German affairs; and then in 1870, France was brought to her knees and forced to yield Alsace-Lorraine. During the Franco-Prussian war, the Swiss sent five divisions under General Herzog to protect the north-west frontier; and as fighting ended, there came the massive problem of interning the 90,000 French troops of General Bourbaki's army of the east who crossed into Switzerland. The miserable plight of the defeated soldiers made Swiss people bitterly resent the jubilation of the German conquerors, and an angry crowd staged a disturbance at a German victory celebration in Zürich.

The Franco-Prussian war was the culmination of the militant nationalist movement in Europe, and brought a tremendous upsurge of chauvinism in Germany. But the Swiss, both in the French and German-speaking cantons, rejected the nationalistic doctrines and stood by their own multi-lingual state with its common purpose and heritage. In general, they took the view that Bismarck was upsetting the balance of power in Europe which they regarded as essential for an effective policy of neutrality. Sooner or later it was likely that they would fall foul of the Iron Chancellor; but it was not until a year before his dismissal by the Kaiser that a serious incident arose, and it was the refugee question that finally caused the trouble. Bismarck was annoyed with Switzerland for giving refuge to German socialists, who he believed were allowed to continue stirring up agitation against his government. He declared that since the Swiss police were inadequate to deal with the situation, Germany would have to organise a police force of its own in Switzerland. The Federal Council would have none of it, and in 1889 abruptly expelled the German police inspector Wohlgemuth sent to spy on refugees. Bismarck was furious. But neither repeated diplomatic protests and threats, nor the abrogation of the agreement facilitating residence and employment for the two countries' nationals, could browbeat the Federal Council into changing its attitude.

Whatever persuaded the Germans to abandon pressure on Switzerland, they must have weighed up the possible international consequences of a breach of the neutrality which the Swiss were determined, and increasingly well prepared, to defend. Switzerland had very good reasons for building up its defensive strength. Its position on vital transit routes across the mountain passes always made it a centre of big power interest, and the new Alpine railways with the longest tunnels in Europe had greatly increased its strategic importance.

During these tests of its foreign policy in the formative years from 1848, Switzerland had at first been meagrely represented abroad. Up to 1867, the country had diplomatic missions only in Paris and Vienna; but in that year an envoy was posted to Berlin, and this was followed by the appointment of representatives to Rome in 1870, to Washington in 1882, and to London in 1891. The establishment of diplomatic links made the Confederation's policy more widely known, and respect was enhanced by the work of the humanitarian organisation so closely identified with Switzerland, the International Red Cross. It was set up in Geneva mainly through the efforts of Henri Dunant, a young businessman who wrote a pamphlet, *Un Souvenir de Solferino*, describing the sufferings he had witnessed in the Italian war of independence. The appearance of Dunant's moving account of the misery of war was followed in 1863 by an historic meeting on aid for wounded soldiers, organised by the Geneva Public Welfare Society and supported among others by the Confederation's most famous military man, Dufour. A year later several countries attended a conference arranged by the Federal Council, and they subscribed to the Geneva Convention on war wounded.

The Red Cross societies which they and other nations formed paid a tribute to Switzerland by adopting as their emblem a red cross on a white ground, the Swiss colours in reverse. Moreover, all members of the International Committee of the Red Cross are Swiss citizens.

About the time of the establishment of the Red Cross, Switzerland's position as a neutral country in the centre of Europe was also beginning to attract other international organisations to its soil. The long list of those which have made their headquarters there in modern times was started with bodies like the International Telegraph Union, the Universal Postal Union, and the International Railway Transport Office. The country was also becoming one of the world's main conference centres. Assemblies without number were held there to discuss the common problems and interests of mankind, and Switzerland took a keen part in such co-operative effort. This was the policy of active neutrality which the makers of the Confederation had in mind. It foreshadowed the day when Switzerland would be chosen as the headquarters of the League of Nations. It also raised a crucial issue for the country in the 20th century, an issue that was to be the subject of profound debate: how far could membership of the League and the United Nations, with provision for sanctions and military action against those accused of aggression, be reconciled with Switzerland's chosen path of permanent neutrality?

II THE FIRST WORLD WAR

The European power struggles of the second half of the 19th century had produced an ominous change in the Swiss situation. In the past, Switzerland had been confronted by France in the west and Austria in the east; to north and south lay the German and Italian states, troublesome but divided. Now, however, the Swiss were completely encircled by big powers, like no other small nation on earth. The old state of affairs had been dangerous enough. The new one could be even more perilous, in view of the rivalries between France and Germany, Austria and Italy.

The conflicting interests of these countries created a highly inflammable situation for all of Europe. France was dreaming of revenge for her lost war with Germany and an opportunity to regain Alsace-Lorraine. Italy had ambitions to push her frontier up to the

Brenner pass and wrest South Tyrol from the Austrian Emperor, Franz Joseph. The Emperor, struggling to hold together the 12 nations of his Danubian monarchy, was under pressure from the Pan-Slav movement encouraged by Russia. Then there was the new united Germany, left behind in the international scramble for colonial possessions and all set now for a brazen grab to make up for what it had missed. In this explosive atmosphere, the international armaments industry was hoping for big and secure profits, while the nations themselves did not yet grasp the catastrophic consequences of a modern war. Overcrowded, restless peoples were living with the threat of a world-wide conflagration. It was ignited in the summer of 1914 by the assassination in Sarajevo of Archduke Franz Ferdinand, heir to the Austrian throne, by a young Bosnian fanatic. The assassin released all the pent-up hatred in Europe. In the slaughter of the next four years more than 10 million people were to die.

The outbreak of war was as great a blow to the hopes and ideals of the neutral Swiss as it was to the peoples of other countries. During the preceding six months, the Swiss had been devoting themselves to the achievements of peace. At the beginning of February, the New Helvetic Society had been founded to promote national interests, as the original patriotic society had done in the 18th century. April had seen the inauguration of new university buildings in Zürich. A few weeks later the National Exhibition at Berne had opened its gates to show the world what could be accomplished by a small country without pretensions to power. And now in summer Swiss troops moved up to protect their frontiers.

The Federal Council informed the powers that Switzerland was resolved to remain "faithful to its centuries-old tradition, not to depart in any way from the principles of neutrality." And it was determined to demonstrate that this neutrality would be defended. The mobilisation on August 3 of the entire army of nearly 250,000 men went without a hitch. This was largely to the credit of the outstanding Chief of the General Staff, Theophil Sprecher von Bernegg. To the people and the Federal Assembly it seemed that Sprecher, a Protestant aristocrat from the Grisons, was the obvious choice for the post of General. But the Federal Council disagreed and prevailed on the Assembly to choose the corps commander Colonel Ulrich Wille. The Assembly finally elected him by 121 votes to 63 for Sprecher.

Wille, born in Hamburg of Neuchâtel stock, was regarded, because of his stern manner, as personifying the Prussian spirit. He had complete faith in the Swiss militia, was responsible for an army reorganisation in 1907, and was considered by the Federal Council as the country's most capable military leader. Since the Swiss manoeuvres of 1912, which the Kaiser had attended, he had also been so regarded by the Germans. He and Sprecher were in many ways contrasting characters. The two officers, so different in appearance and background—Wille red-faced, sturdy and forthright, Sprecher austere, lean and sharp-featured—nevertheless set an example of conscientious co-operation throughout the war.

Hardly had popular feelings over the contested choice of General simmered down when a much more serious division became apparent, and one that raised fundamental questions about Swiss nationhood. The division arose from conflicting sympathies with the belligerent powers, and it threatened to tear the nation apart. The French-speaking Swiss regarded the German attack on Belgium as a violent blow against peace, liberty and the dignity of man. In their eyes Britain and France were right to warn the smaller countries that this was what they would have to expect from the nation whose anthem proclaimed "Deutschland über alles." But large numbers of German-speaking Swiss admired and believed in Germany. Many Swiss intellectuals had absorbed the culture of German universities; and German scientists, teachers and industrialists were playing a prominent role in northern Switzerland. The number of Germans there was in fact so large that linguists were seriously suggesting the Swiss vernacular might disappear within three generations and that by the year 2000 Basle and Zürich would speak the same German as Frankfurt and Berlin.

Although by no means all the Swiss allowed themselves to be carried away by partisan attitudes to the war, the gulf was serious and getting wider. The Confederation could be enriched by a balance of German, French and Italian cultural influence, and could count on the very diversity of its society as an element of strength. But this depended on tolerance and an underlying unity. When loyalties were confused by the appeal of nationalism from across the borders, and particularly German nationalism, Switzerland's very existence was threatened. The federal government, the responsible press, and thoughtful opinion in the country were aware of the danger of the gulf becoming permanent. That is was bridged was due in great measure to the intervention of one of German-speaking Switzerland's great poets, Carl Spitteler.

As Gottfried Keller had spoken for Swiss liberalism during the times of trial in the 19th century, so now Carl Spitteler called on the people to remember where their loyalties lay in the confusion of 20th-century Europe. He appeared before an audience in Zürich on 14 December 1914, and appealed for reason, tolerance, unity and a true understanding of what Swiss neutrality meant. For Spitteler, then nearing 70, it was in some ways a reluctant intervention by a poet in the realm of politics, undertaken in the first place at a suggestion from the New Helvetic Society. But it was all the more effective coming from a respected and eminent man like Spitteler, especially when he declared that the loyalty the Swiss owed to each other was immeasurably greater than any attachment they felt to the people of another nation. "We must realise," he said, "that our political brother is closer to us than the best neighbour and racial kinsman. To strengthen this realisation is our patriotic duty. It is not an easy duty. We must feel united without being similar."

If neutrality of opinion was a difficult matter to define, the obligations of a neutral in other respects had been laid down in the Hague agreement of 1907. The export and transit of arms was permitted, and so was the passage of wounded and sick through neutral territory. But troops and supply columns of the belligerents were not allowed to pass. After the German invasion of Belgium, however, it was clear that the military strategists cared little about the barriers of international law unless neutrality was shielded by a strong army. The possibility of a drive through Switzerland to outflank the enemy was something the strategists had always taken into serious consideration. The north-west of Switzerland bordering France and Germany was the area most vulnerable to attack; and it was here on the line of the Jura from Basle to Les Rangiers that three Swiss divisions were concentrated, with three more held in reserve. Defensive measures elsewhere included strengthening the natural bastion of the St. Gotthard with barrier forts and reinforcing the south-eastern frontier. The latter became especially important when Italy's entry into the

Henri Dunant (1828–1910), originator of the International Red Cross, established in Geneva in 1864. In 1901, Dunant was awarded the Nobel Peace Prize.

Clockmaking—a traditional craft and still one
of Switzerland's key industries.

A masterpiece of modern road engineering—
and, deep down below, a mountain village
that has seen many changes in Alpine
communications. The picture shows the
southern approach ramp to the Gotthard pass
near Motto Bartola.

The Federal Assembly meets to elect the Federal General, the commander-in-chief of the army, who is appointed only in times of emergency. The date here is 30 August 1939. The choice falls on Henri Guisan, the popular officer who symbolized the country's determination to maintain its independence.

war against the central powers completed the ring of fire around Switzerland's borders.

Four-fifths of the thousand violations of the Swiss frontiers during the war were due to over-flights, and the powers made no direct threat of invasion. But Swiss troops, who exchanged their dark-blue uniforms for field-grey, had to keep constantly alert for trouble. The long months of armed inaction proved how right General Dufour was when he once said it was more difficult for troops to endure this sort of thing than to show bravery in battle. It was not until after the war that men came to appreciate the positive side of it, the comradeship, the physical fitness, the chance to get to know people of different social backgrounds from all parts of the country. War-time military duty was in this sense a unifying force; and the Swiss in general fulfilled their active service, averaging about 500 days, with goodwill and devotion.

This loyalty of ordinary people made them all the more resentful over two breaches of neutrality by men at the very top in Swiss military and political life. The first case, in 1916, involved two colonels of the general staff. They were found to have regularly supplied the German and Austro-Hungarian military attachés with confidential bulletins concerning the military operations of the belligerent powers. The affair caused an uproar, and both the colonels were suspended from their posts. A year later, in the spring of 1917, there was a much more serious case, involving none other than Switzerland's Foreign Minister—Arthur Hoffmann, the Federal Councillor in charge of the Political Department.

Hoffmann, in his eagerness to show that Switzerland could do something to bring peace to a war-weary world, violated the established rule that any peace mediation by a neutral power must be simultaneously addressed to both sides. The incident arose when a young socialist member of the Swiss National Council, Robert Grimm, went to Petrograd after the Russian revolution and then cabled Hoffmann asking about the possibility of talks to end hostilities. Hoffmann's despatch in reply was intercepted by the Russians, and revealed that he intended to pave the way from Berne for a separate peace between Russia and Germany. The western powers were indignant; they naturally reckoned that if the Germans no longer needed to worry about their eastern front, they would

reactivate their offensive in the west where it had become bogged
down in trench warfare. Hoffmann, who had omitted even to inform
his own colleagues on the Federal Council of his action, had no
option but to resign.

Hoffmann's successor at the head of the Political Department was
72-year-old Gustave Ador of Geneva. He was highly regarded both
for his long record of political service and for his work as president
of the International Red Cross. The Red Cross and its army of volunteers played a tremendous part in Switzerland's humanitarian work
during the war. Prisoners of war were put in touch with their families,
help was given in exchanging the seriously wounded and sick, and
tens of thousands of people evacuated from war zones were allowed
to cross Switzerland into safer areas of their own countries. Sick
prisoners were welcomed to Switzerland for convalescence, and in the
last two and a half years of the war the Confederation looked after
about 68,000 internees. Among them were 1,500 students who were
given the opportunity of attending Swiss universities. After the war
the Swiss offered hospitality to 40,000 Austrian children, mainly from
Vienna, who were in need of recuperation.

Economically, the war had found Switzerland ill prepared. In
August 1914, the country had only a few weeks' bread supply, and
after that the imports and exports by which it lived were at the mercy
of the belligerent powers. They were all determined to prevent food-
stuffs, raw materials and other goods reaching their enemies through
Switzerland, and they therefore insisted that it should submit to strict
checks on its foreign trade. These were carried out by two semi-
official organisations—"The German Goods Control Trustees" in
Zürich and the "Société Suisse de Surveillance Economique" whose
initials S.S.S. were bitterly interpreted as "souveraineté suisse suspen-
due." When in 1917 Germany began to wage an unrestricted U-boat
campaign in reply to Britain's naval blockade and the United States
threw its power and its shipping into the allied war effort, food and
raw material supplies from overseas became even scarcer in Switzerland. Home-grown produce was inadequate to make up the balance,
and food rationing had to be intensified. The bread coupon, introduced in October 1917, allowed daily emergency rations of half a
pound of bread per person. Towards the end of the war the government also brought in potato rationing.

Food shortages, rising prices, low wages and resentment of war profiteers fanned the discontent of the workers, who blamed militaristic capitalism for the war. This bitterness brought about a major political crisis involving the Swiss Social Democratic Party. After its foundation in 1870, the party had followed a moderate socialistic policy, and although recognising the concept of the class war it adapted international Marxism to Swiss conditions. But the moderate leadership had lost control by 1914, and during the war the party became increasingly revolutionary, encouraged by foreign agitators among the political refugees in the country. Lenin spent three years in Berne and Zürich before his return to Russia in 1917, and he was the spiritual leader of the socialist congress at the Bernese villages of Zimmerwald and Kiental in 1915–16 which laid the foundations for the Third International, the Comintern, dedicated to the establishment of international communism. Lenin's revolutionary triumph in Russia in 1917 was hailed enthusiastically by the Swiss proletariat, and many Swiss socialists felt that the hour of revolution had struck for them as well. For although the Social Democratic Party had been represented in the National Council since 1890, socialists were growing disillusioned with parliamentary methods. Since the rise of the trade unions in 19th-century Switzerland, the workers had often seen the strike weapon pay dividends. Now there were demands for its drastic use to deal a blow to the existing order.

The climax came at dawn on 11 November 1918. The day of armistice in the west, 12 months after Lenin's revolution, saw the outbreak of the Swiss general strike. Four-hundred-thousand workers joined in. To deal with the emergency, the Federal Council called out troops; and on 12 November the Federal Assembly met in extraordinary session. The Assembly backed the Federal Council's immediate measures and also moved towards a compromise solution. It declared its support for certain political and social reforms by constitutional methods. The strike leaders were called upon to order a return to work, and the following day they gave in.

The main reforms introduced after the general strike were the eight-hour day and a system of proportional representation for electing the National Council. This latter change broke the traditional grip of the Radicals and gave the Social Democrats a much greater share in Swiss parliamentary democracy. In the 1919 elections, the

Social Democrats increased their number of seats in the National Council from 19 to 41; and in later years they were to become the strongest party, although they had to wait till 1943 before they obtained their first seat on the Federal Council.

In the immediate post-war years, the Social Democratic Party stuck to revolutionary principles. But later it gradually dropped the more extreme Marxist demands, and by the mid-thirties was developing the policy of evolutionary socialism confirmed since the second world war at the 1959 party congress at Winterthur. The party never joined the Third International, and because of this the extreme left-wing broke away to form a Communist Party. The Communists were banned during the second world war but when the ban was revoked in 1945 they re-emerged as the Labour Party. Since 1918, the trade unions have never again been involved in a general strike, and in modern times have resorted to the strike weapon less and less. The Swiss Federation of Trade Unions has sought to improve the living standard of the workers within the framework of the democratic system, in concert with such organisations as the consumer co-operative movement, to which nearly half the Swiss families belonged by 1948.

The general strike of 1918 was thus a turning point in Swiss political development. In the years to come it led to a closer association between the socialist movement and the democratic life of the state. The major party of the left shed its extremists and became a powerful partner in the government.

1 2

Europe and the Dictators

I THE LEAGUE OF NATIONS

"**N**O MORE war!"—But first the settlement. Germany, charged as the aggressor, was made to pay. It surrendered territory in all directions, incurred huge debts in reparations, and had its military power shackled. The Rhineland was demilitarised; France regained Alsace-Lorraine. In the Danube area, the Habsburg empire finally disintegrated and new states emerged. Austria and Hungary were separated and cut down in size. Italy advanced to the Brenner pass, taking over South Tyrol.

The collapse of the Austrian empire gave a chance to the people of Vorarlberg, adjoining eastern Switzerland, to proclaim their right to self-determination; and in 1919 they voted overwhelmingly in favour of union with the Confederation. To them the move promised peace and order. But the Swiss had misgivings about the admission of a 23rd canton. Although there was some sympathy for the aspirations of Vorarlberg, it was decided that it would be unwise for Switzerland to gain territory at the expense of defeated Austria. So this westernmost frontier of Austria remained unaltered. However, Switzerland did conclude an enduring customs and postal union with the small principality of Liechtenstein, which sought the arrangement to replace its former economic links with Austria.

When Germany and Austria had been dealt with by the allied powers, it was still an open question what sort of order would be established in the world. "No more war!" had been the cry from battlefields, parliaments, churches and the stricken towns of Europe. But if peace was to last, international goodwill and security were essential. Neither the neutrals nor the defeated states had a seat at the Paris peace conference; yet all were affected by the idealistic principles laid down by the American President, Woodrow Wilson. The hopes of peoples everywhere were bound up in the Covenant of the League of Nations which, thanks to the President, was placed within the framework of the Treaty of Versailles. When the headquarters of the League was chosen, neutral Switzerland became more closely associated than ever before with the course of international affairs. For the choice was Geneva, the city of Calvin, Rousseau and the Red Cross.

By now Switzerland had a long record of active participation in international bodies. It wanted to help to unite mankind, and it had a natural self-interest in making the world safe for smaller states. But the League's early evolution was already turning out to be something of a disappointment, and the path to Swiss membership was strewn with doubts and misgivings. All the Federal Councillors were decidedly in favour of joining. The National Council, too, supported the idea by 128 to 43, and the Council of States voted for it by 33 to 6. The Councillors felt that the decision, the most vital in the Confederation's history, must be submitted to the popular vote. A referendum was therefore organised, in which majority support would be required both in the nation as a whole and among the cantons.

All over the country supporters and opponents of League membership argued heatedly at public meetings. Those in favour asserted that the idea of federation, which had brought freedom and peace to Switzerland was now being adopted by the international community, and it was therefore the Confederation's moral duty to co-operate. Refusal would mean hopeless isolation. But many thought otherwise. The opponents of League membership included the farmers, with their dislike of unfamiliar ideas; the socialists to whom the League was a "capitalist concern"; and some of the most senior officers, such as Wille and Sprecher. They emphasised that the League was in fact not a world-wide organisation. The United States was refusing to join, despite all the efforts of Woodrow Wilson; and Germany and Russia were excluded. In the eyes of the opposition, it was turning out to be an organisation dominated by the victorious European powers. And as such, would it not give rise to German demands for a counter-league?

This, indeed, was seen to be the central issue : was it permissible for a neutral state to take sides in advance? And what was the attitude of the League of Nations towards Switzerland's permanent neutrality? This controversial question was cleared up by the Declaration of London of 13 February 1920. The Council of the League recognised that Switzerland's neutrality was consistent with League principles. The Confederation would not be bound to take part in military sanctions and would not have to permit the transit of foreign troops for operations against an aggressor nation. It would, however, be called upon to join in any economic sanctions the League might apply.

Though these assurances made it easier for many Swiss to vote in favour of joining the League, the result of the referendum on 16 May 1920 was uncertain until the last moment. Ten and a half cantons had said "yes" and an equal number "no," while the Grisons was still counting the returns from its mountain communes. Then, at last, relief in Geneva: "Les Grisons acceptent!" The popular vote throughout the Confederation went in favour of entry by 415,000 to 323,000, chiefly because of the massive support of French-speaking areas like Vaud which registered 63,300 in favour to 4,800 against. The people of Switzerland had taken an historic decision on a major principle of foreign policy.

These were once again great days for Geneva. Switzerland gave especially active support to the social and humanitarian work of the world community and to efforts to establish the rule of law. It was represented in the League for 20 years by its Foreign Minister from the Ticino, Guiseppe Motta, who twice presided over the Assembly, and as a brilliant linguist was on close terms with many of the visiting foreign statesmen. Motta was one of the great personalities of those days in Geneva, listened to with respect if not always with agreement. A controversial aspect of his policy was his opposition to the admission of the Soviet Union to the League. Switzerland had had no diplomatic relations with the Soviet Union since shortly after the October Revolution. In November 1918, it expelled the Soviet envoy and his staff because of Bolshevik propaganda. After this, the Swiss legation in Petrograd was looted, and official relations between the two countries were severed. In 1923, the Russian diplomat Worowsky, who was accredited to Italy, was murdered in Lausanne. At the trial, the local jury found the accused, Conradi, guilty by five votes to four, but because of the large dissenting vote he could not be punished under Swiss law. As a result, the Russians declared an economic boycott of Switzerland by decree of 20 March 1923. Although Swiss commercial and industrial circles, as well as many workers, would have liked to see a resumption of normal relations, this did not come about because of Motta's negative attitude.

Motta's views about the Germans and the League were quite different: he pleaded strongly for them to be allowed to join. They finally did so in 1926 but their membership did not last long. The Weimar Republic had been battered by the disastrous financial crisis of the early twenties, when even in Switzerland 146,000 people were out of work, and within a few years it was to crumble under the massive burden of six million unemployed. By 1933 Hitler was in power, taking Germany out of the League and the Disarmament Conference. The danger to Europe was becoming clear, and the League, as it slowly disintegrated, carried less and less conviction as an instrument of peace-keeping. Faith in its ability to establish a system of collective security began to diminish, and small nations like Switzerland questioned the protection it could give them. The Swiss were now in the unenviable position of having both Nazi Germany and Fascist Italy as neighbours.

After Mussolini's rise to power from 1922 onwards, Switzerland had done its best to maintain a correct relationship with Italy. A great test of this policy came in 1935 when the League decided to impose sanctions against Italy for its attack on Abyssinia. Switzerland partly complied but argued that its neutral position made it impossible to carry out a policy of unqualified sanctions against a neighbour. It rejected an all-out boycott of Italian goods and operated an arms embargo against both Italy and Abyssinia, a compromise which aroused strong protests from other League members. The affair underlined Switzerland's dilemma as a permanent neutral, neighbour of the dictators and a member of a League of Nations which was steadily losing authority, not least because of the policies of the great powers. In this situation, the federal government came to the conclusion that it must revert to the policy of absolute neutrality. In due course, the League Council formally recognised that Switzerland, because of its neutral position, was unwilling to continue the application of sanctions and the Council agreed not to call on the Swiss to do so in future. The League's statement was dated May 1938, two months after Hitler had swallowed up Austria and only four months before the Munich Agreement by which Czechoslovakia was sacrificed to him.

II THE SECOND WORLD WAR

The world was all too slow to realise the danger of Hitler, despite the clear threats in his book *Mein Kampf* and his violent propaganda. National Socialism, he declared, was the answer to the German people's yearning for security and honour after the shame of Versailles, and it would eliminate their enemies, the Jews and the Communists. On his rise to power in 1933, Hitler broke the spirit of the German élite and crushed all opposition as he ruthlessly laid the foundations of the new Reich that was intended to endure for a thousand years, the empire of the master race uniting everyone of German blood. Within the next decade the swastika was indeed hoisted on such outposts of the new realm as the Acropolis, the mountains of the Caucasus, and the deserts of North Africa.

To the Swiss Confederation, the Nazi racial cult was not only repugnant: it was a direct menace, from just across the border, to the whole basis of Switzerland's varied and multi-lingual society. The Führer seemed like the hated *Vogt*, a throw-back who was bringing ferocious modern techniques to the ancient evil of enslaving peoples and trampling on the rights of the individual. From the days of the Habsburgs, the Swiss had always resisted autocratic rule, and their modern constitution gave expression to their hatred of it. They held with Pestalozzi that the state needs humanising, not worshipping. Yet here were the Germans making Hitler their idol—spellbound, it seemed, by the mass rallies and the armed might of the Nazi fatherland. Small countries, like minority groups, could expect no sympathy from the new Reich: according to the German geo-politician, Haushofer, they were just by-products of history.

Not all the Swiss, however, were immune to the magic of Nazism. Young people in particular, many of them bored with the pettier issues of democratic politics, were often enthralled by the new "supermen." There were power-seekers, too, in Swiss society who hoped that by joining the march of National Socialism they would be swept into the leadership of a new Switzerland united with Germany. Attempts were made to soften up the Confederation for an assault by the Nazis, and their propaganda methods were used to back up a campaign for joining the German Reich. A pro-Nazi movement was formed, the *Nationale Bewegung der Schweiz*. Anti-semitic agitation went on, and there was an attempt to ban the freemasons as Hitler had done in Germany. But these moves foundered on the commonsense of the majority of the Swiss people; and as the Nazis were to admit, their campaign had no effect on the nation as a whole.

The argument for union with Germany received an answer from the Swiss when the Nazis invaded Austria in March 1938 after softening it up with propaganda. Within a week, the Federal Assembly unanimously proclaimed its determination to preserve Switzerland's independence. Later in the year, after Hitler had stripped Czechoslovakia of the Sudetenland with its important frontier defences and industries, the Federal Council issued a declaration reaffirming what Swiss policy stood for : the unity of the Confederation and its democratic institutions, the liberty of the citizen and faith in western civilisation. The following March the Nazis overran the whole of Czechoslovakia, showing what they thought of such ideas. It was a tragic outcome to the appeasement policy of the British Prime Minister, Neville Chamberlain, and his Munich Agreement with Hitler under which the Sudetenland had been sacrificed. Switzerland's attitude to Munich was summed up in a speech by a member of the Federal Council, Hermann Obrecht. "We Swiss," he declared, "will not start making pilgrimages abroad."

These years saw a powerful revival of Switzerland's unity, and the political indifference that had been prevalent in the twenties was put aside. In the face of the Nazi challenge, democracy could no longer be taken for granted as an accepted political fashion : it was now a matter of survival, and the situation made it imperative to win over the younger generation to a full understanding of the ideals of the Confederation. The people closed ranks regardless of political allegiance, social status, religion or language. The German-speaking population took even greater pride in their Schwyzertütsch the more the literary tongue was debased by Nazi propagandists; and when the Fascists claimed that Romansh was simply an Italian dialect, the Swiss people in 1938 voted massively in favour of giving it the status of their fourth national language. The deliberate emphasis on Swiss culture at this time did not mean that the country was turning its back on the rest of the European tradition. Indeed, that could not happen in a multi-lingual society with free access to information about the affairs of other countries. There was thus no risk that the pride in Swiss achievements shown at the National Exhibition in Zürich in 1939 would lead to dangerously inbred attitudes. But the exhibition did enable people to renew their faith in their country and to take fresh heart in a time of crisis.

Before the National Exhibition closed, the second world war had begun. On 1 September Poland was attacked by the Nazis. All over Europe men were called to arms, and after the years of waiting it came as no surprise. Switzerland had used those years to strengthen its army thoroughly. A defence bill had been passed; and although in the first world war the Social Democratic congress had voted against national defence, leading socialists had now come to support it in the realisation that the fulfilment of their hopes depended on maintaining an independent Switzerland. The days before war broke out were given over to a series of emergency moves. On 28 August the frontier defence troops were called up. On the next day the Federal Council declared a state of active service throughout the country. On 30 August the Council was given emergency powers, and the Federal Assembly elected the popular Henri Guisan of Vaud as General by 204 votes out of a total of 229. Twenty-four hours later, the Federal Council issued a proclamation that Switzerland would abide by its traditional neutrality. General mobilisation and an order for labour conscription followed quickly.

After Hitler's three-week campaign against Poland came six relatively uneventful months. Then the Nazis pounced on Denmark and Norway, and a few weeks later the blitzkrieg was raging in Western Europe. Hitler's armies swept through the Netherlands, Belgium and Luxembourg, outflanking and finally breaching the French Maginot Line, and forcing Britain to evacuate her troops from Dunkirk. Mussolini's Italy chose its moment to join the victorious Germans: the Vichy government of France abandoned military resistance. At the fall of France, thousands of French and Polish troops made their way into Swiss territory, where they were interned.

Switzerland was now an isolated democracy in a Europe of dictatorship, exposed not only to possible attack but to the danger of fifth column subversion which had contributed to the astonishingly swift collapse of other countries under Nazi pressure. The Federal Council therefore declared: "Any reports disseminated by radio, leaflet or other means which seek to cast doubts on the determination of the Federal Council and the army to resist aggression should be regarded as enemy propaganda lies. Switzerland will resist to the utmost with all means at its command."

Nevertheless, in the critical month of May 1940, with Germany triumphant in the West, there were many people whose resolve to defend the country had been shaken and who drifted into an attitude of defeatism. The man in the street could hardly believe his ears when on 25 June 1940 he heard Swiss ministers make an astonishing broadcast urging the people to "discard the old attitudes." Dangerous advice it sounded, in the light of the incessant German propaganda calling for allegiance to the "new Europe."

But there were still leaders who rejected compromise and defeat. General Guisan was one of them. At the end of July 1940, a month after the bewildering ministerial broadcast, he summoned his senior officers to the Rütli meadow in order to draw fresh inspiration from the "mysterious call of the past" which came from the place where the original pact of 1291 was signed. To his officers, and to the people, he issued a call to stand firm and show their determination. The significance of the call, and the place from which it was made, was not lost on the people. It was followed by a tremendous upsurge both of national morale and of Guisan's popularity as a leader.

Guisan was convinced that it was vital to preserve the heartland of the country at all costs, and that this was more important in the event of attack than defending every inch of territory at heavy loss. The major change of strategy which this concept implied meant that instead of preparing to defend the frontiers the army concentrated its strength on the fortified Alpine area—the national redoubt—which would be held even if other parts of the country had to be sacrificed. The redoubt, to be defended if necessary until the whole nation could be liberated, became a living symbol of Switzerland's will to resist. This will was strengthened by the patriotic organisation known as *Heer und Haus* (Army and Home) which encouraged idealism and steadfastness and helped to combat the danger of subversion. To demonstrate that the spirit of the nation was not to be undermined, both the Nazi front and the Communist Party were banned :

in its dangerous situation Switzerland could not tolerate groups which owed their first loyalty to foreign countries.

As well as being prepared to defend themselves, the Swiss had also to sustain their economy. Before the outbreak of war, the Economic Department under Hermann Obrecht had made sure that the granaries were filled and that Switzerland would not be open to blackmail by threats of starvation. Now as much food as possible had to be produced by the Swiss themselves. Under the plan devised by Professor Wahlen, the farmers set about bringing more and more land under the plough and increasing productivity. The country, normally so dependent on exports and imports, managed to avoid having its trade completely strangled by the dictators; and although it was forced to do business with them, it also found ways of exporting goods to the allies.

One lesson that Switzerland had learned from the first world war was that proper provision had to be made for the families of soldiers on active service. The arrangements during the 1939–45 period made life much more tolerable than it had been in the first war, for servicemen received payments out of a wages compensation fund, to which employers, employees, the federal state, and the cantons all contributed. As a result of these measures, there were few to whom siding with Germany seemed the solution to economic difficulties. But, as in every other nation, there were people in Switzerland who caved in under the pressure of war or allowed themselves to be bribed into spying and sabotage. Eighteen persons were convicted by military courts for such offences and sentenced to death : seventeen of them were executed. Another fourteen were sentenced to death in absentia, but after the war these sentences were commuted to life imprisonment.

The constitution lays down that every Swiss is obliged to do military service, and never was the principle more effectively observed than during the war. In September 1939, under the first general mobilisation, 400,000 men were called up. After the second mobilisation order of May 1940, half a million were under arms. But with the inclusion of auxiliary services, home guards and the women's services, more than 850,000 were engaged in the defence of their country. On average there were never less than 100,000 men under arms at any given time. Again, as in the first world war, it was a question of waiting for attack; but a small number of airmen who went up to drive foreign intruders out of Switzerland's skies were killed in combat. To begin with, the intruders were mostly German. Later, after the Royal Air Force had beaten off the Luftwaffe assault across the Channel and the United States had joined the war against Germany, Swiss air space was chiefly violated by allied flyers. More than once bombs fell on towns in northern Switzerland. The worst incident occurred on 1 April 1944 when 40 people were killed at Schaffhausen on the Rhine during a daylight raid. In this tragic affair, the American pilots were misled by the city's proximity to German territory and by difficulties of navigation in bad weather.

After the United States and the Soviet Union had entered the war in 1941, the dictators were without hope of ultimate victory. By 1943 the democracies, triumphant in Africa, were poised to invade Italy, and the Fascist regime was beginning to totter. It was about this time that Switzerland seemed most in danger. Communications from north to south were now more than ever important to Hitler; and in March 1943 the Swiss intelligence service reported that a German move against Switzerland was imminent. The Nazis probably reckoned that if they were in complete command of the Alps they might stand a better chance of resisting an Allied onslaught on central Germany. Hitler may also have feared that the Allies would themselves try to seize the Swiss Alpine redoubt as soon as they were in a position to do so.

In view of the intelligence reports about German plans, General Guisan took the unorthodox step of meeting the German General Schellenberg. During this encounter, at an inn at Biglen near Berne, Schellenberg was left in no doubt that Switzerland was determined to resist aggression. When, in the late summer of 1943, Mussolini's empire collapsed, the Germans carried on the fight in Italy, and Switzerland was more than ever hemmed in by Hitler's armies. But the Führer knew that if he were to attack the Swiss "hedgehog," bristling with Alpine defences, he would tie down more of his forces than any potential gains would warrant. Besides, the use of the Gotthard line for the transport of coal supplies was clearly more valuable to him than a chain of ruined installations, since the Swiss would undoubtedly have blown up the Gotthard tunnel if he had invaded.

Looking back, the Swiss realise that all their military and economic precautions would not have sufficed to save them from the fate of so many European countries had the Nazis decided to strike. As it was, the moment of worst danger passed, and all initiative in the war was falling from Hitler's grasp. In the early summer of 1944 the Americans and British successfully invaded Normandy, and from then on Germany was relentlessly forced back. On 8 May 1945 the Third Reich collapsed, in the thirteenth of Hitler's promised thousand years. The wailing of the air raid sirens stopped. Church bells rang out the cease fire. All Europe was at last released from the stranglehold of the Nazi dictator.

13

Switzerland Since 1945

I THE INTERNATIONAL COMMUNITY

SWITZERLAND'S POLICY of permanent neutrality had secured it both peace and internal stability for 100 years and had seen it through two world wars in which it might have been dismembered. The question now was how the policy would serve the country and the cause of European harmony in the very different circumstances of the second half of the 20th century.

During the war the Confederation had fulfilled more than 40 mandates from belligerent states to look after their interests in territories controlled by their enemies. The fighting men and prisoners of war had been helped by the Red Cross to the utmost of its ability, while tens of thousands of refugees had been received in Switzerland despite the danger of overcrowding in a small country facing the problem of economic survival. The federal and cantonal governments and private citizens gave generously to finance aid for the peoples who suffered in the war. One of the most striking examples of this humanitarianism was the *Schweizerspende*, under the direction of **Rodolfo Olgiati**, in which all Swiss efforts to assist those in need were co-ordinated and which helped to save thousands of European children from starvation. Another example was the children's aid action of the Swiss Red Cross, which during and shortly after the war provided three month holidays in Switzerland for 150,000 needy boys and girls.

After Hitler's grip was broken the Confederation was able to resume full relations with the countries of Europe and the world beyond, seeking to do so, as the Federal Council said, in a brotherly spirit. Switzerland's neighbours were impoverished and exhausted, great powers no longer. They had fought their battles, and among the younger generation in particular there was a yearning to have done with war and start out on an era of co-operation among western countries. The new division in Europe coincided with the line of partition in Germany. The new power blocs were those dominated by the Soviet Union and the United States, a situation soon reflected in the United Nations and the movements for regional defence and co-operation.

Recognition of the changed power structure was implicit in Switzerland's decision to seek a restoration of diplomatic relations with the Soviet Union, broken off since 1918. The Swiss took the initiative in November 1944; but their approach was turned down by the Russians, who were strongly critical of Switzerland's foreign policy and obviously still nursed a grievance over the opposition by the pre-war Foreign Minister Giuseppe Motta to Soviet membership of the League of Nations. It was not until March 1946 that the two countries finally agreed to establish legations, and later embassies, in each other's capitals.

When the United Nations came to be set up on the basis of the wartime alliance, both the Soviet Union and the United States were founding members, and this fact alone marked out the new organisation from the old League. Political realities were also acknowledged by giving the big powers permanent seats in the Security Council, which was intended to enable the United Nations to act more swiftly and effectively against breaches of the peace than the League. But the requirement of big power unanimity for decisions on important issues meant that any of them could veto action, as the Soviet Union frequently did in the growing atmosphere of cold war. Small countries resented the big power dominance; yet more and more of them joined the United Nations, making the General Assembly their forum and invigorating the work of the U.N.'s special agencies.

The very first General Assembly of the United Nations decided to buy the old League of Nations building and to make Geneva its European headquarters. Nevertheless, Switzerland was one of the few countries which did not apply to join the United Nations. It remained outside in such mixed company as the two Germanies and Communist China, though for entirely different reasons. The Swiss people's vote to join the League had been a narrow one, but the League did make concessions to Switzerland's policy of permanent neutrality. The United Nations system of collective security was felt

to be incompatible with the Swiss policy, and there was little inclination among the people to change a course which had produced the
most stable frontiers in continental Europe in order to join a United
Nations in which peace-keeping and disarmament were crippled by
big-power dominance and disharmony.

Switzerland has, however, played an active part in the United
Nations system as a sympathetic non-member. Its foreign policy,
guided in the post-war years by Federal Councillor Max Petitpierre,
followed the principle of neutrality and solidarity. In this spirit, the
country joined those specialised international agencies which have no
political overtones and do not conflict with its neutrality. It continued membership of the older organisations of this type still in
existence, such as the International Labour Organisation, as well as
the new International Court of Justice. It also became an active
member of such important U.N. agencies as the World Health
Organisation, the Food and Agriculture Organisation, and the United
Nations Educational, Scientific and Cultural Organisation (UNESCO);
and it has made big contributions to the U.N. International Children's
Emergency Fund (UNICEF). It also belongs to the General Agreement on Tariffs and Trade (GATT) which, like the W.H.O. and
I.L.O., has its headquarters in Geneva.

The role the Swiss play in the United Nations system is also
demonstrated by their share in assisting the developing countries. In
1969, they were among only six advanced nations to reach the U.N.
target of devoting at least 1 per cent of their gross national product
to aid, although most of the funds involved came not from the state
but from private sources. Considerable capital has been made available to the World Bank, and a White Paper issued by the Federal
Council on 30 June 1969 declared that Switzerland would consider
joining the World Bank and the International Monetary Fund.

These moves indicate that Switzerland's leaders are clearly aware
of the desirability for the closest association with those organisations
whose activities increasingly mould the international scene and
directly affect Switzerland's own destiny. The 1969 White Paper,
which ran to 175 pages, contained a detailed analysis of the country's
relations with the United Nations, and in fact threw the whole question of membership wide open to further discussion. Although the

report still held that Switzerland could not immediately see its way to becoming a full member, the very detail of the Federal Council's examination of the problem showed that the attitude is in no sense one of indifference but a conscientious doubt about the compatibility of United Nations membership with the Swiss policy of permanent neutrality.

II EUROPEAN INTEGRATION

The rebuilding of Western Europe after the second world war led to a degree of co-operation unknown before, spurred on by the threat of Communism. The establishment of the European Coal and Steel Community in 1952 was followed six years later by the creation of the European Economic Community linking France, West Germany, Italy, Belgium, the Netherlands and Luxembourg. Instead of being surrounded by mutually hostile powers, a situation to which its neutral foreign policy had been adapted, Switzerland found itself encircled by a new and constructive alliance, the Common Market. The country's great neighbours, the old enemies of innumerable wars, were now allies in a co-operative venture for peaceful progress, as well as being defence partners of the United States in the North Atlantic Treaty Organisation.

Switzerland has joined neither NATO nor the Common Market. In the case of the western defence alliance, the reasons are obvious; but membership of the E.E.C. also raises problems for the Swiss. In order to join the Common Market, they would have to abide by the Treaty of Rome which envisages not only an economic but also a political community to which Switzerland feels it could not subscribe because of its policy of permanent neutrality. Nevertheless, it has welcomed the way its neighbours have tried to sink their differences for a common purpose, and as a country vitally dependent on international commerce its aim has been to encourage economic co-operation and to work for conditions of freer trade. To that end it joined the Organisation for Economic Co-operation and Development and the European Free Trade Association, which was founded the year after the establishment of the E.E.C. and linked Switzerland with Britain, Austria, Denmark, Norway, Sweden and Portugal. Since the spring of 1963, Switzerland has also been a full member of the Council of Europe in Strasbourg, which deals with a variety of matters of common concern but excludes defence.

The Swiss blend of representative and direct democracy means that the country's future relations with either the United Nations or the E.E.C. are not simply a matter for government and policy-makers. Public opinion cannot be told what is good for it. The debate cannot be confined to the columns of the newspapers or the floor of the Federal Assembly. A change in Switzerland's policy in these vital matters would have to be put to the popular vote and receive majority support among the people and the cantons.

III THE POLITICS OF COALITION

In Swiss politics today, there are three big parties, a smaller one with considerable influence, and several minority groups. The big parties, which have roughly equal strength in the Federal Assembly at Berne, are the Radicals, the Social Democrats and the Conservative and Christian Social Party. Federal government depends not on the formation of temporary coalitions as in some other multi-party states, with shaky political alliances put together for the sake of electoral convenience, but on continuing co-operation among the parties in the cause both of national stability and of harmony between the Confederation and the cantons. Under the Swiss system, government is permanently representative of the major political forces which have developed from the diversity of life in the Confederation : it is very much a coalition of political interests with no party powerful enough to override the others.

This tradition is reflected in the continuity and composition of the governing Federal Council, whose seven members are drawn from all the main parties and whose term of office is dependent on their willingness to serve rather than on the marginal fluctuations of political fortunes at election time. The convention nowadays is that the Radicals, the Social Democrats and the Conservatives each have two members on the Federal Council; the seventh member comes from the next strongest party in the Confederation, the Farmers', Artisans' and Citizens' Party.

Switzerland has therefore evolved a coalition system with none of the instability which has characterised coalitions in other countries.

It is a system of give and take suited to the temperament and traditions of the Swiss people and to the unity amid diversity which is the Confederation's great strength. The multi-party nature of the country's political life is shown in the composition of the Federal Assembly. After the elections of 1967 the seats in the National Council and the Council of States were distributed as follows, the position after the previous elections in 1963 being shown in brackets:

National Council (200 members elected nationally by proportional representation)
Radicals: 49 (51)
Social Democrats: 51 (53)
Conservative and Christian Social Party: 45 (48)
Farmers', Artisans' and Citizens' Party: 21 (22)
National Association of Independents: 16 (10)
Liberal Democrats: 6 (6)
Democratic and Protestant Peoples' Party: 6 (5)
Labour Party (formerly Communist Party): 5 (4)
Others: 1 (1)

Council of States (44 members, two from each canton)
Radicals: 14 (13)
Social Democrats: 2 (3)
Conservative and Christian Social Party: 18 (18)
Farmers', Artisans' and Citizens' Party: 3 (4)
Liberal Democrats: 3 (3)
Democratic and Protestant People's Party: 3 (3)
National Association of Independents: 1 (0)

The Federal Council

The seven members of the Federal Council, their political parties, their cantons of origin, and the government departments for which they are responsible (1970) are as follows:

Pierre Graber (Social Democrat, Vaud): Political Department
Ludwig von Moos (Conservative, Obwalden): Justice Department
Hans Peter Tschudi (Social Democrat, Basle): Interior Department
Ernst Brugger (Radical, Zürich): Economic Department
Roger Bonvin (Conservative, Valais): Transport and Power

Rudolf Gnägi (Farmers', Berne): Defence Department
Nello Celio (Radical, Ticino): Finance Department

The Parties

The cantonal structure of Switzerland is reflected in the way its parties are organised. In broad outline, they are not national parties but federations of local party organisations. Bearing in mind the importance of this cantonal foundation, here is a brief sketch of the political line-up.

The *Radicals* were the great party of Swiss liberalism in the 19th century, dominating the country's politics and opposed only from the right. But with the introduction of proportional representation in 1919, they lost their position of dominance and also found themselves yielding the initiative in various social matters to the Social Democrats. In the new situation they became the party of the centre, shorn of some of their former huge following in the country but still a strong partner in its political affairs.

The *Social Democrats* were the party to benefit most from proportional representation, and have progressed to being the biggest party in the National Council with membership of the Federal Council since 1943. Their earlier Marxism has given way to evolutionary socialism, widening their appeal among the middle class. They are now the party of social reform and a mixed economy.

The *Conservative and Christian Social Party,* formerly the Catholic Conservatives, derives from the Catholic Party of the 19th century first organised to oppose radicalism and centralism. It draws its main strength from the old Catholic and mixed cantons, still supports cantonal rights against over-centralisation, and is the biggest party in the Council of States. As the chief conservative group in the country, it stands as the champion of individual rights and liberty, but in reflecting the modern social teaching of the Catholic Church it has been taking a more liberal attitude to measures of social reform.

The *Farmers' Party* entered the Federal Assembly after the introduction of proportional representation in 1919, and achieved membership of the Federal Council 10 years later. Its main support comes from the farming community, whose interests it keeps in the eye of both the public and the government.

The *Liberals*, mainly Protestant and nowadays broadly conservative in their political attitudes, have declined from their influential position in the 19th century. But modern times have seen the rise of one new vocal group in Swiss politics, the *National Association of Independents*. This was organised by one of the characters of modern Switzerland's public and commercial life, the entrepreneur Gottlieb Duttweiler, who before his death was head of the country's first supermarket chain. The Association of Independents stands boldly for the defence of consumers' interests and strongly opposes state intervention. It is not a member of the Federal Council, and likes to regard itself as the only effective opposition in a country of continuing coalition. Its campaigning style brought it the biggest gains of all the parties taking part in the 1967 elections.

IV   THE MODERN ECONOMY

From modest beginnings, Switzerland has built up a highly industrialised economy, with a foreign trade turnover among the biggest in the world in relation to population. Swiss products are sold in more than 100 countries. Over 10 per cent of total exports go to the United States, and about the same proportion to Asia. But Switzerland's main trading area is obviously Western Europe, and particularly the surrounding countries of the European Common Market. In 1968, 59.4 per cent of Swiss imports came from E.E.C. countries, and 35.9 per cent of its exports were sold to them. The comparable percentages for the smaller European Free Trade Association were lower at 16.5 and 21.2 per cent; but Switzerland attaches great importance to E.F.T.A. trade, and its rate of growth has been greater than with either the E.E.C. or the rest of the world. One result of creating the Free Trade area has been that Switzerland diverted 41 million dollars worth of its purchases from third countries to its E.F.T.A. partners.

Swiss industry has traditionally concentrated on supplying specialised quality products, and specialisation is the key to the country's modern economy. The emphasis is on industrial products of advanced technical design and consumer goods of the highest standards. With little in the way of domestic natural resources, other than the vital water power which drives thousands of hydro-electric stations throughout the country, industry has geared itself to processing imported raw materials and semi-manufactured goods. The greater part of the resulting finished products go for export, and this enables industry to exploit economies of volume production despite the small domestic market. The skill which is put into the production process makes "Made in Switzerland" a sign of added value and reliability in world markets.

The country's main industries, in order of their contribution to the economy, are machinery and metal working, chemicals and pharmaceuticals, watch-making and textiles. All sell a very high proportion of their products abroad : the pharmaceutical and watch-making industries export more than nine-tenths, and the chemical and engineering industries about two-thirds of their output.

The manifold branches of machine production and metal working employ more people than any other industry and account for about a third of the country's total exports. Beginning in the early days with textile machinery, the output now includes turbines, diesel engines, locomotives, electrical and hydraulic equipment, and farm machinery, all of a high technological standard. Thousands of firms are engaged in the industry, the greatest among them being Sulzer Brothers and the Brown, Boveri company, both of which have been built up from traditional family businesses into famous international concerns.

The chemical industry, under the leadership of such world-famous firms as Geigy and CIBA, has made tremendous strides in the present century. The dyestuffs side, with its headquarters in Basle, grew out of the needs of the Swiss textile industry and is now one of the main suppliers to the textile trade throughout the world. From this branch there developed the pharmaceutical industry, which has grown so rapidly that the value of its exports now exceeds that of dyestuffs. The whole industry does extremely well in foreign markets, and in 1968 one-fifth of the country's total exports consisted of chemical products.

The oldest Swiss industries, watch-making and textiles, continue to demonstrate their resilience. Watch-making, now third in the export list, still employs thousands of highly-skilled workers; and closely allied to it are jewellery firms and others making radio and optical equipment. The textile industry, like those in other countries, has seen its ups and downs in the face of changing fashion. But it has adapted itself to the age of synthetic fibres, while hundreds of factories specialise successfully in the traditional fields of wool, cotton, silk, rayon and linen, some of them maintaining pre-eminence in their sphere.

The clothing industry has grown up from the textile trade, and now challenges it in importance to the country; and in footwear manufacture the firm of Bally has won a world-wide reputation. Other famous firms are to be found, of course, in the food industry, renowned for its cheese, chocolate, condensed milk and preserved foods. The biggest among them is Nestlé, which accounts for 20 per cent of all Swiss chocolate production.

Exports and imports are vital to Switzerland, and freedom of trade is of the greatest importance to it. But despite the success of Swiss industry and the fame of its products, an excess of imports over exports is a normal feature of the country's economy. This is not the matter for concern it might be thought, however, because the trade deficit is outweighed by invisible earnings which despite their name play a prominent part in the Swiss balance sheet. Income from tourism is the main single contributor under this heading: the tourist industry employs about 140,000 people and the income from it is worth about 250 francs per head of the Swiss population. Even more significant in their way are the earnings that flow from Switzerland's business links. Investments abroad are producing a fast-growing income, which includes the earnings from the foreign subsidiaries of big firms like Brown, Boveri and Nestlé. Insurance earnings are also on a large scale, since Switzerland is the biggest insurer in continental Europe and the biggest reinsurer in the world. On top of this there is the income derived from banking services, with Switzerland the financial centre of the continent, a position it owes in great degree to its economic strength and overall stability.

V THE PEOPLE AT WORK

The transformation of Switzerland into a leading industrial and commercial nation is strikingly reflected in the changing population structure and the way people earn their living. The total population has increased since 1850 from 2,390,000 to over 6,000,000. By

1960, the year of the last census, the population of the towns had risen from about 154,000 to 2,300,000. About half of this urban population lives in five cities with more than 100,000 inhabitants, led by Zürich with nearly 440,000 and followed in order of size by Basle, Geneva, Berne and Lausanne. The census figures of 1960 also showed that nearly half the working population was engaged in industry and manual trades like building, while about a third was working in administration, commerce and banking, the professions, the service industries and the tourist trade.

The number of people employed in agriculture is now relatively small, fewer than one in ten of the working population. Of the industrialised European countries, only Britain and Belgium have an even lower proportion of agricultural workers. However, with larger families than other sections of the population, the Swiss farming community makes up a bigger part of the nation than the figures suggest. Now as in the last century, the rural influence is also reflected in the decentralisation of industry and the appeal the countryside still has for industrial workers : of the 15,000 employed at the Brown, Boveri works at Baden, for instance, only half live near at hand, and the rest travel from country communes as far away as 45 miles. The fall in agricultural manpower has naturally been accompanied by increased mechanisation on the farms, and productivity has been raised by more than a third in the past 30 years. The country's farms still provide most of the people's needs, and in 1968 agricultural products accounted for only 13 per cent of total imports.

On the labour front there are two outstanding features of the modern Swiss economy. One is the virtual absence of strikes. From 1965 to 1967 there were only five strikes in all, affecting a total of 126 workers and resulting in the loss of 1,915 working days. For this situation, which is even more remarkable considering the condition of full employment in the country, the Swiss are undoubtedly indebted to the so-called Peace Agreement of 19 July 1937. In this agreement between employers and workers in the engineering and metal-working industries, both sides bound themselves to waive militant methods in negotiation, to bargain as equals in good faith and to accept conciliation procedures within the enterprises, all state intervention being excluded. The original two-year peace arrangement —a milestone in Swiss industrial history—has been repeatedly renewed for five years at a time, and other industrial sectors followed the example of the engineering and metal-working branches.

The social and economic climate of Switzerland, of course, was ripe for this experiment, and many years of economic prosperity have helped to make it work. Such has been the prosperity and expansion of the economy that labour has been in extremely short supply, and this has produced another remarkable phenomenon: the huge numbers of foreign workers in Switzerland. In August 1969 there were 659,000 of them—almost a third of the total labour force. By far the greatest number were Italians, giving many towns and villages a Mediterranean air as they took their leisure in the evenings; but there were also thousands of Spanish workers, as well as Germans, Austrians and other nationalities. Apart from Federal Germany, which has ten times the population, Switzerland has the highest absolute number of foreign workers anywhere in Europe, a fantastic change from the days when the Swiss had to go abroad to seek a living as mercenaries, farmers or merchants. The availability of foreign workers has been of considerable importance in strengthening the economy. But because their presence in such force also inevitably poses sensitive social and political problems, it has been felt that the number should be kept within bounds, and there has been some decrease in the second half of the 1960's.

By the yardstick even of its prosperous neighbours in Western Europe, Switzerland enjoys a very high standard of living. Gross national product per head of population is second in Europe only to Sweden, and since 1945 the economy has grown at an average rate of four and a half per cent. Although the cost of living has more than doubled in the past 25 years, real incomes have risen a great deal faster than prices. There has been a still greater narrowing of class differentials, which in any event have never been so marked in Switzerland as in some other industrial countries. The Swiss worker was never an industrial proletarian: now with a five-day week and holidays with pay, he is even more on terms comparable with those of people in other occupations.

The Swiss have always been a thrifty people given to personal savings and insurance, and this indeed has been one of the country's strengths. In recent decades, however, the extension of public health services and comprehensive old-age insurance has meant that people no longer have to rely exclusively on their savings, and the socially weaker members of the community are provided for by welfare legislation. Since 1948, Switzerland has had a federal insurance scheme, with the Old Age and Dependents Insurance Act entitling everyone to a modest old-age pension linked to income and also providing for widows and orphans. Both the old-age and disability insurance schemes are contributory and compulsory, and benefits have been increased steadily to take account of the higher cost of living. It is widely felt, however, that benefits ought not to be so large as to constitute a full national old-age pension. Most Swiss still feel that apart from state and vocational group insurance, everyone should try to save and retain the incentive to build up some capital or alternatively take out voluntary insurance. Health and accident insurance, for instance, are still largely voluntary, although both receive federal financial support and several cantons have made such insurance compulsory.

VI   CONCLUSION

Modern Switzerland has not only witnessed improvements in the standards of social welfare; the quality of life as a whole has changed. Visible symbols of this are the tall buildings that have taken the place of two-storey estates in many parts of the country, the vast increase in motor traffic with nearly every family owning some sort of vehicle, the new national motor routes financed mainly from federal funds, and developments such as the construction of the St. Bernhard tunnel, which in 1967 at last provided the mountainous Grisons with an efficient round-the-year route from north to south. Perhaps the most significant monuments to scientific change are the atomic power stations: in 1969 one of them, at Beznau, was already operational and two more were being built as the forerunners of the most vital future source of power for industry.

Nobody, however, can pretend that today's changing society has no drawbacks. Switzerland, like other countries, provides enough evidence to the contrary. To take two obvious examples: modern traffic has destroyed the peace of many a rural area; modern factories, office blocks and homes, desirable though they are, have given rise to more waste and industrial effluent, polluting many rivers and lakes. There are also examples in the daily lives of the people. The Swiss are no more immune than others from the worst features of television entertainment, the materialism of the consumer society, or the complacency of affluence. Such aspects of modern life often cause acute concern, among the educated young in particular. In Switzerland, as elsewhere, the student generation has shown signs of restlessness and frustration, seeking outlets for the sense of idealism and adventure which it often finds lacking in today's efficient, highly-organised state. Some of the shortcomings of modern society have been highlighted by Switzerland's most distinguished contemporary dramatists, Max Frisch and Friedrich Dürrenmatt. Both have taken their fellow-countrymen to task for petty attitudes and parochialism. But both have recognised that the deep-seated problems of the 20th century have a universal character, and it is this that has given them a wider stage in dealing with such issues as war, totalitarianism, and the dangers of the scientific civilisation.

Twentieth-century developments have focused attention on certain important questions in Swiss political life. Direct democracy is weakened by the fact that relatively small numbers of people bother to vote on some issues, and there are those who maintain that the values of Swiss democracy are being debased by consulting the people on too many topics too frequently, particularly where technical matters are involved which the layman can hardly be expected to judge adequately. Coalition government also has its critics, who stress that to function properly a democratic system needs effective political opposition. Then, in its industrial structure, Switzerland resembles other advanced countries in showing an unmistakable tendency towards economic associations and mergers. Large organisations make sure they are represented on parliamentary bodies so that their voice is heard; and by virtue of their power they often exert a dangerous influence in political affairs.

The constitutional relationship between the cantons and the federal state is another matter of continuing debate. In general terms, the federal state's authority has been considerably strengthened over the years, and some see this trend as an unwelcome diminution of cantonal responsibility. The state has long been the country's largest employer; it is assuming many new commitments; and it is finding the means to do so in the revenue from the prospering economy, including the federal defence income tax which was originally introduced as a wartime measure and has been retained despite the constitutional tradition of reserving direct taxation to the cantons. It is worth noting, nevertheless, that in 1969 the Federal Government still only had a one-third share in total public finance.

One sphere in which the cantons' autonomy is still considerable is education. Yet even here, they are having to take account of the centralising trend, in the interests of the children. For with increasing population mobility, every Swiss child on average moves home at least once in his early school days. The new school may well be in a different canton with a different kind of teaching system, and these changes in methods cause many children a great deal of trouble. Efforts are, therefore, being made to achieve some co-ordination among the various cantonal education schemes. Already in university education, the federal state is providing considerable subsidies to the cantons without infringing their rights, while they are being encouraged to co-ordinate their research and teaching programmes. Thus in education, as in other matters, the tendency is in the direction of further strengthening the federal state and limiting cantonal autonomy. Indeed, there is continuing discussion in parliament, the cantons, the universities and elsewhere of the idea that the federal constitution should undergo a total revision to reflect this general trend towards centralisation. At the same time, there is opposition in the country to excessive central control.

Whatever solutions are found to internal problems of this sort, and to the questions arising from the country's relations with its European neighbours and the United Nations, the decisions will be based on the Swiss tradition in public affairs at communal, cantonal and federal level and can only be understood on this historical basis. Winston Churchill, in a speech in Zürich in September 1946, drew a moral from the success of the Swiss people in achieving unity based on tolerance and overcoming the differences of race, language and customs between the numerous cantons. In Switzerland, he said, politics was a civic task and not a question of power; and in this the country was an example to others. The point is still worth stressing : the Swiss have an ingrained faith in mutual help and solidarity, and their political system, with its direct democracy, enables everyone to bear a share of responsibility in the running of the country. They are also united in insisting that their lives should be governed by the rule of law and not by force. They reject autocrats at home and abroad; and their profound belief in liberty found renewed expression in numerous protest meetings against the Soviet invasion of Czechoslovakia in August 1968, and the granting of political asylum to more than 10,000 Czechoslovak refugees in the following 12 months.

Since 1815 Switzerland's frontiers have been more stable than those of any other continental country. Its role as a neutral has been positive and constructive; and the good works of its citizens, exemplified by the Red Cross, have been a token of national goodwill. As a multi-lingual nation, the Swiss do not disparage the languages of other peoples, but learn and like them. Divided between Protestants and Catholics, they have acquired the virtue of tolerance, and the Pope's visit in 1969 to Geneva, the city of Calvin, was in this sense a symbolic act in the movement towards religious reconciliation in the Christian world.

The essential secret of Switzerland's peace and freedom is thus the ability to maintain a fair balance between all the component elements of its society. On this theme, Federal Councillor Wahlen spoke for the Swiss people when he once said: "Whether we look upon it as an achievement or a favour of providence, it is true that the peaceful co-existence within our borders of peoples and languages representing a large part of Europe is both a miracle and an example worthy of imitation. To us, at any rate, it must continue to serve as a model for the future shape of Europe." The Swiss are seeking to apply their principles in a practical way less by attending great conferences than by offering a helping hand from man to man and nation to nation. They believe this is perhaps the best way of creating a new spirit without which any international order will remain a soulless shell.

The Swiss Cantons

The cantons and half-cantons are here listed in the order in which they joined the Confederation, the dates of entry being given in brackets. The percentages of population, according to language and religion, are based on the last official census of 1960. A new census is to be held in 1970. Population totals are estimates based on data for 1967 and 1968.

URI (1291): One of the four forest cantons (*Waldstätte*) clustered around Lake Lucerne (Vierwaldstättersee), whose Everlasting Alliance of 1291 was the foundation of the Confederation. Uri lies on the southern tip of the lake, in the central region of the Alps, on the approach to the Gotthard and the south. Its capital is Altdorf (pop. 8,400), with monument to William Tell. Area of canton: 415 sq. miles. Population: 33,500 of whom 94.5 per cent are German-speakers and 92.5 per cent Catholic.

SCHWYZ (1291): The forest canton that gave its name to the country; in the town of Schwyz (pop. 12,300) the archives contain the document of the original alliance. The canton lies north of Uri, is mainly pre-Alpine, and its area is 350 sq. miles. Population: 85,000. German speakers: 94.3 per cent; Catholics: 93.6 per cent.

OBWALDEN (1291): One of the half-cantons of Unterwalden, the other being Nidwalden. Both these forest cantons preserve the ancient tradition of the *Landsgemeinden*, the popular assemblies which are the foundation of Swiss democracy. Obwalden's capital is Sarnen (pop. 6,600); its area is 190 sq. miles; its population 25,200. German speakers: 96.2 per cent; Catholics: 96 per cent.

NIDWALDEN (1291): The smaller part of Unterwalden; area: 107 sq. miles; capital town: Stans (pop. 5,000), where the great educationist Johann Heinrich Pestalozzi cared for the orphans after the

French onslaught of 1798. Population: 25,000 of whom 93.5 per cent are German speakers and 92 per cent Catholic.

LUCERNE (1332): First of the towns to join the confederates, after being a Habsburg possession. The town (pop. 74,400) is situated at the north-west corner of the lake on both sides of the river Reuss, which is spanned by several bridges including the awning-covered Kapellbrücke, dating from 1333. Lucerne's location has always made it an important commercial and transit centre on the Gotthard route from the north to Italy, and it is also a major tourist town. Cantonal area: 576 sq. miles. Cantonal population: 281,000. German speakers: 94.3 per cent. Catholics: 85.1 per cent.

ZÜRICH (1351): Switzerland's most populous canton (pop. 1,084,000) and biggest city (pop. 436,000); achieved economic supremacy with its silk, cotton and engineering industries, its commerce, banking and insurance. Abounding in intellectual life, with the Federal Institute of Technology and university; birthplace of Pestalozzi, the 19th-century writers Gottfried Keller and Conrad Ferdinand Meyer, and of the modern novelist and dramatist Max Frisch. Centre of Ulrich Zwingli's work in the Swiss reformation, and of democratic progress in the last century. Protestants make up 65.8 per cent of the canton's population, and 88 per cent are German speaking. Cantonal area: 667 sq. miles.

GLARUS (1352): Another of the old cantons which preserves its *Landsgemeinde,* Glarus lies east of Schwyz, is traversed by the river Linth, and is rich in remote Alpine scenery. Economic prosperity came with cotton spinning and cotton printing, and other industries followed textiles. The capital is the town of Glarus (pop. 6,100), to the north of which lies Näfels where the men of Glarus defeated the Habsburgs in 1388. Cantonal area: 264 sq. miles. Population: 42,100. German speakers: 86.9 per cent. Protestants: 58.8 per cent.

ZUG (1352): North of the forest cantons, partly pre-Alpine, partly plateau; its capital, the town of Zug (pop. 23,100) extends from the lake of the same name, was the site of pre-historic settlement, has a wealth of medieval remains, and its modern industries include engineering and metal-working. Cantonal area: 93 sq. miles, which makes it the smallest of all the full cantons. Population: 65,000, of which 90.4 per cent are German-speaking and 83.1 per cent Catholics.

BERNE (1353): Capital of the Confederation, seat of federal government and also of international organisations. The city (pop. 168,700) was founded in 1191 by Duke Berchtold of Zähringen, became a free imperial city, and in later times extended its dominion over a wide area until the French invasion of 1798. Its history is preserved in fine old streets and buildings, grouped in a loop of the river Aare as it flows through the plateau. Cantonal population: 994,000. German speakers: 80.5 per cent. French speakers: 14.4 per cent. Protestants: 79.9 per cent. It is the second biggest canton: 2,657 sq. miles.

FRIBOURG (1481): In the plateau of the south-west, this is a borderland between French-speaking and German-speaking Switzerland, and is subject to the cultural influences of both languages. Of the cantonal population of 172,000, French speakers make up 63.4 per cent, German speakers 34 per cent and 86.3 per cent are Catholics. The town of Fribourg (pop. 40,000) is another 12th-century foundation of the Zähringen family. Cantonal area: 645 sq. miles.

SOLOTHURN (1481): Linking the plateau and the Jura in the north-west. The town of Solothurn (pop. 19,000) was a Roman settlement, became a free imperial city in the 13th century, and was the residence of the French ambassador at the time in the 17th and 18th centuries when the Confederation concluded mercenary service agreements with France. The town is the centre of an industrial area with watch and instrument making, engineering and textiles. Cantonal area: 305 sq. miles. Population: 226,000. German speakers: 90.3 per cent. Catholics: 57.7 per cent.

BASLE TOWN (1501): On both banks of the Rhine at the meeting point of Switzerland, Germany and France, and thus a major communications centre and river port. Basle is also an important commercial, financial and industrial city, famous for its development of the silk trade and after that of chemicals—now its main industry. Its university, founded in 1460, is the oldest in Switzerland. Its famous mayor, Rudolf Wettstein, secured the Confederation's legal independence from the Empire in the Peace of Westphalia of 1648. The city population is 215,000, and the area of the half-canton 14 sq. miles. German speakers: 89.4 per cent. Protestants: 59.8 per cent.

BASLE COUNTRY (1501): The half-canton of the rural areas which separated from the city in 1833. The capital is Liestal, a town of 11,300 people. Area: 165 sq. miles. Population: 194,100. German speakers: 88.1 per cent. Protestants: 65.3 per cent.

SCHAFFHAUSEN (1501): The town of Schaffhausen (pop. 38,300) lies on the right bank of the Rhine, not far from the German border and just above the Rhine Falls, the greatest waterfall in Europe. In the area of the canton there was pre-historic settlement. The town grew up round an 11th-century monastery, gained in commercial importance, and in modern times its industries include metal working, engineering, textiles and precision instruments. Cantonal area: 115 sq. miles. Population: 72,700. German speakers: 91.1 per cent. Protestants: 71.4 per cent.

APPENZELL, Outer Rhodes (1513): The mainly Protestant half-canton divided from Appenzell Inner Rhodes in 1597 on religious grounds. Of the population of 50,500, Protestants make up 76.6 per cent and German speakers 93 per cent. The area is 94 sq. miles, and the capital is Herisau (pop. 15,400).

APPENZELL, Inner Rhodes (1513): Mainly Catholic (96.2 per cent) and also German-speaking (95.8 per cent). The old town of Appenzell (pop. 5,400) is another that keeps alive the tradition of the *Landsgemeinde*. Area: 67 sq. miles. Population: 13,500. Both the half-cantons are surrounded by the canton of St. Gallen in the pre-Alpine area of eastern Switzerland.

ST. GALLEN (1803): The town of St. Gallen is the biggest in eastern Switzerland (pop. 79,600) and hub of the region's economic life. It grew around the monastery founded in the 7th century by the Irish monk Gallus, and became an important cultural influence with a monastery school celebrated for its scholarship and often regarded as a forerunner of Europe's universities. Traditional centre of Swiss textiles, employing more people in the industry than any other canton. Educational establishments include the Graduate School of Economics and Administration. Cantonal area: 697 sq. miles. Population: 375,000. German speakers: 93.3 per cent. Catholics: 61.9 per cent.

GRISONS (1803): The biggest canton in Switzerland (2,746 sq. miles) and the most sparsely populated in proportion to area (pop. 153,000). In the Alpine region of the south-east, it is a land of tourism, mountaineering and winter sports. It is also the region of the Romansh language, spoken by 26.1 per cent of its population. German is spoken by 56.6 per cent and Italian by 16.1 per cent. Protestants and Catholics are almost equally divided. The cantonal capital is Chur (pop. 30,200), and other centres are those noted as tourist resorts such as Davos and St. Moritz.

AARGAU (1803): Canton in the northern plateau through which runs the Aare, the longest river entirely within Switzerland (183 miles), on its way to join the Rhine. The towns along the river include the cantonal capital Aarau, an industrial centre (pop. 17,700), with the headquarters of the famous Bally shoe concern a few miles away at Schönenwerd. On the river Limmat is Baden, a watering place since Roman times. Cantonal area: 542 sq. miles. Population: 417,000. German speakers: 90.5 per cent. Protestants: 52.4 per cent.

THURGAU (1803): In north-east Switzerland, extending from the southern bank of Lake Constance into the plateau and pre-Alpine areas. The capital Frauenfeld (pop. 17,500) is an important market centre for the agricultural districts. Area: 388 sq. miles. Population: 187,000. German speakers: 91.7 per cent. Protestants: 60.9 per cent.

TICINO (1803): The main Italian-speaking canton (88.2 per cent) lying on the southern side of the Alps and taking its name from the Ticino river. Parts of it were brought under confederate control in the 15th century and more in the Milanese campaigns of the early 16th century. It became a canton under Napoleon's Act of Mediation in 1803. Its capital is the town of Bellinzona (pop. 16,200) a few miles from Lake Maggiore, the northern tip of which lies within Swiss territory. Cantonal area: 1,086 sq. miles. Population: 237,000 of whom 91.2 per cent are Catholics.

VAUD (1803): Extending north from Lake Geneva; and mainly French speaking (79.2 per cent). Established as a canton after emerging in 1798 from a long period of Bernese dominion. Capital is Lausanne (pop. 139,200), rising from the lake-side, a commercial centre and resort and also the seat of the Federal Tribunal, the highest court in the country. Cantonal area: 1,239 sq. miles. Population: 502,000, of whom 70.7 per cent are Protestants.

VALAIS (1815): The valley of the Rhone runs for more than 90 miles through this southern canton, with its traditional wine and fruit growing. Its cultural and historic development has been influenced by the Romans, the Germanic tribes and the French, who annexed it during the Napoleonic wars because of the importance of the Simplon pass. Its capital, lying on the Rhone, is the town of Sion (pop. 21,400), a place of both Celtic and Roman settlement, an early bishopric whose most celebrated bishop was Matthäus Schiner, leader of the campaigns against the French in the early 16th century. The canton has an area of 2,020 sq. miles with a population of 191,000; it is 95.9 per cent Catholic, and is divided in language, 61.7 per cent French and 33.6 per cent German.

NEUCHÂTEL (1815): The Jura mountains rise westwards from Lake Neuchâtel, the area of which has provided archaeological evidence of prehistoric lake dwellings and of the Celtic civilisation associated with La Tène, the site on the north bank. In more modern times, Neuchâtel became a principality of Prussia in 1707; and although it joined the Confederation in 1815, it was not until 1857 that Prussia finally relinquished its claim to the territory. The canton is famous for its watch-making industry. The cantonal capital of Neuchâtel (pop. 36,700) lies by the lake and is an important cultural centre. Cantonal area: 309 sq. miles. Population: 166,000, of whom 78.3 per cent are French-speaking and 68.5 Protestant.

GENEVA (1815): The city of Geneva (pop. 172,100), situated where the river Rhone leaves the lake, is the centre of international organisations, European headquarters of the United Nations, birthplace of the Red Cross, Rousseau and Calvinism, and a focus of

the watch-making craft. A Celtic settlement, it was conquered by
the Romans, later became a free imperial city and was long in
conflict with Savoy. Its cultural tradition is French and the language division of the canton is 70.0 per cent French, 13.3 per cent
German and 9.6 per cent Italian. Protestants and Catholics are
about equally divided. Total area : 109 sq. miles. Cantonal population : 318,300.

Table of Dates

ca. 100,000 years B.C.: First inhabitants of Switzerland make their appearance in the caves of the Appenzellerland, the Oberland of St. Gallen and other regions.

ca. 15,000 B.C.: Cave dwellers of the Jura near Schauffhausen.

ca. 3000–1800 B.C.: Swiss lake villages of the Neolithic period.

from 500 B.C.: La Tène culture of the late Iron Age Celts: the Helvetii in west and north Switzerland.

58 B.C.: Caesar defeats the Helvetii at Bibracte: the beginning of Roman rule.

ca. A.D. 260: The Germanic Alemanni destroy the city of Aventicum.

ca. A.D. 500: Alemannian settlement begins, in the shadow of Frankish power.

ca. A.D. 600: The Christian mission of St. Columbanus: the monks of St. Gallen.

A.D. 800: Charlemagne, King of the Franks, crowned in Rome by Pope Leo III; Switzerland under the Holy Roman Empire.

ca. 1200: St. Gotthard pass opened up: the Alpine valleys link the trade routes.

1231: The community of Uri wins important privilege: directly subject only to the Empire.

1240: Similar status for Schwyz: both communities free of Habsburg control.

1273: Rudolf of Habsburg becomes Emperor. Secret alliance between Uri, Schwyz, and Nidwalden.

1291: Death of Rudolf. Uri, Schwyz, Nidwalden (and later Obwalden) conclude their Everlasting Alliance.

1315: Battle of Morgarten: Swiss confederates defeat the Habsburgs, then renew their alliance in the agreement of Brunnen.

1332 : Lucerne joins the Confederation.

1339 : Battle of Laupen : victory for Berne and the confederates.

1351 : Zürich joins the Confederation.

1352 : Glarus and Zug also join.

1353 : Berne joins : *the eight-community Confederation.*

1386 : Battle of Sempach : Swiss victory over the Habsburgs.

1388 : Glarus triumphs in the Battle of Näfels.

1393 : Covenant of Sempach : confederate military agreement.

from 1414 : Council of Constance meets to deal with Church schism. Expansion of the Confederation in north and south; Aargau and Ticino areas occupied.

1436–50 : Civil war against Zürich, aided by Austrians and French mercenaries. Battle of St. Jakob an der Birs (1444) turns the tide for confederates.

1460 : Further expansion : Austrians driven out of Thurgau. University founded at Basle.

1476 : War against Burgundy : Swiss defeat Charles the Bold at Grandson and Morat.

1481 : Covenant of Stans resolves post-war disputes between town and country : the intervention of Niklaus von Flüe. Fribourg and Solothurn join the Confederation.

1489 : Hans Waldmann, burgomaster and dictator of Zürich, arrested, condemned and executed.

1499 : Swabian War : de facto independence from the Empire.

1501 : Basle and Schaffhausen join the Confederation.

1513 : Appenzell joins : *the Confederation of 13 cantons.*

1500–16 : Milanese campaigns : victory at Novara (1513), defeat at Marignano (1515), the beginning of neutrality.

1519 : Ulrich Zwingli in Zürich : start of the Swiss reformation.

1531 : War with the Catholic cantons. Zürich defeated, Zwingli killed.

1536 : Calvin in Geneva.

1545–63 : Council of Trent : counter-reformation begins.

1618–48 : Thirty Years War. Peace of Westphalia gives legal recognition to Switzerland's independence.

1647 : Defensionale of Wyl : confederate defence agreement.

1653 : Peasant rising in Switzerland; leaders executed.

1663 : Mercenary service agreement with France.

1712 : Peace of Aarau resolves further religious conflict.

1749 : Rebellion in Berne : rebel leader, Samuel Henzi, executed.

1761 : Foundation of the Helvetic Society, dedicated to national regeneration. Members include Johann Heinrich Pestalozzi.

1762 : Jean Jacques Rousseau (born Geneva, 1712) publishes *The Social Contract*.

1777 : Mercenary agreement with France reaffirmed.

1789 : Revolution in France.

1792–93 : Massacre of the Swiss Guards in Paris : Louis XVI executed.

1798 : The French occupy Vaud, Fribourg and Solothurn. Berne falls. The end of the old Confederation.

1798–1803 : The Helvetic Republic : the new unitary state.

1803 : Napoleon's Mediation Act settles civil strife, establishes *Confederation of 19 cantons,* including St. Gallen, Aargau, the Grisons, Thurgau, the Ticino, and Vaud.

1815 : Napoleon defeated at Waterloo. Congress of Vienna : Geneva, Neuchâtel and the Valais join *Confederation of 22 cantons.* Big powers guarantee Switzerland's territory and recognise its permanent neutrality. Restoration and reaction in Switzerland under Federal Pact.

1830 : July revolution in Paris.

1831 : New liberal constitution in Zürich followed by other cantons.

1841 : Religion and politics lead to conflict in Aargau and Lucerne.

1845 : Catholic cantons form the Sonderbund.

1847 : Civil war against the Sonderbund.

1848 : Revolution in Europe. The new Federal State in Switzerland, with democratic institutions.

1857 : Prussia renounces all claims to Neuchâtel.

1859 : Confederation prohibits recruitment of mercenaries.

1860 : France annexes Savoy.

from 1863 : Basle Country and Zürich take the lead in drive for more direct democracy.

1863–64 : Emergence of the Red Cross : first Geneva Convention.

1870 : Franco-Prussian war : 90,000 French troops interned.

1874 : Revision of the constitution, with greater centralisation.

1898 : State control of the railways.

1914 : World war : the poet Carl Spitteler reminds the Swiss of their duties as neutrals.

1918 : War ends. Swiss general strike.

1919 : Proportional representation introduced for National Council elections.

1920 : Switzerland joins the League of Nations after neutrality assurances and referendum.

1923 : Russia declares economic boycott of Switzerland : diplomatic relations already severed.

1935 : Swiss dilemma over sanctions against Italy.

1939 : Second world war.

1940 : General Guisan calls on Swiss to stand firm, organises Alpine defences.

1946 : Relations with Russia restored.

1950 : Switzerland joins Organisation for European Economic Co-operation (later O.E.C.D.).

1959 : Switzerland a member of the European Free Trade Association.

1963 : Full member of the Council of Europe.

1969 : Federal Council White Paper on relations with the United Nations.

Select Bibliography

I *English*

Bonjour, E., H. S. Offler, G. R. Potter: *A Short History of Switzerland* (Oxford, Clarendon Press, 1952).

Bonjour, Edgar: *Swiss Neutrality* (London, Allen & Unwin, 1946).

Codding, G. A.: *The Federal Government of Switzerland* (London, Allen & Unwin, 1961).

Gilliard, Charles: *A History of Switzerland* (London, Allen & Unwin, 1955).

Hughes, Christopher: *The Parliament of Switzerland* (London, Cassell, 1962).

Hughes, Christopher: *The Federal Constitution of Switzerland* (Oxford, Clarendon Press, 1954).

Imlah, Ann J.: *Britain and Switzerland, 1845–60* (London, Longmans, 1966).

Martin, P. E.: *The Swiss Confederation in the Middle Ages* (Cambridge, Cambridge Medieval History, VII; 1932).

Martin, William: *A History of Switzerland* (London, Grant Richards, 1931).

Natan, Alex, ed.: *Swiss Men of Letters.* Essays on "The Four Literatures of Switzerland" with bibliography (London, Oswald Wolff, 1970).

Rappard, William: *Collective Security in Swiss Experience, 1291–1948* (London, Allen & Unwin, 1948).

Schürch, Ernest, ed.: *Switzerland; Life and Activity* (London, Allen & Unwin, 1953).

Soloveytchik, George: *Switzerland in Perspective* (London, Oxford University Press, 1954).

II *Other languages*

Calgari, Guido: *Die vier Literaturen der Schweiz* (Olten, 1966).

Fueter, Eduard: *Die Schweiz seit 1848* (Zürich, Orell Füssli, 1928).

Guggenbühl, Gottfried: *Geschichte der Schweizerischen Eidgenossenschaft* (Zürich, 1947).

Martin, William: *Histoire de la Suisse* (Lausanne, Payot, 1963).

Nabholz, H., L. v. Muralt, R. Feller and E. Bonjour: *Geschichte der Schweiz* (2 vols., Zürich, 1932–38).

v. Salis, J. R.: *Schwierige Schweiz*. Beiträge zu einigen Gegenwartsfragen [Essays] (Zürich, Orell Füssli, 1968).

Index